Irish Travellers,
Culture and Ethnicity

- Section on Nomadism when you write about trad Tp life
  see p 97 -
- I mis'judged the social aspects of Nomadism,
  focused on econ. O/w see it as being so v. impt
  to Tp identity once they settled / housed.
- Also, anthro-training made me reluctant to call their
  travel "Nomadism" bec it was diff from
  Nomadic H & G.

  We called it itinerancy. Loaded term. Negative
  when Nomadism has / implies culture, garners
  respect. Itinerancy is like homelessness, a
  social problem. Shift in terminology has
  made a difference.

Published 1994
The Institute of Irish Studies
The Queen's University of Belfast,
Belfast

This book has received support from the Cultural Traditions Programme
of the Community Relations Council, which aims to encourage acceptance
and understanding of cultural diversity.

British Library Cataloguing-in-Publication Data. A catalogue record for
this book is available from the British Library.

ISBN 0 85389 493 0

Printed by W & G Baird Ltd., Antrim
Cover designed by Rodney Miller Associates
Photography by Derek Speirs

Irish Travellers:
Culture and Ethnicity

Edited By

May McCann

Séamas Ó Síocháin

Joseph Ruane

Institute of Irish Studies,
The Queen's University of Belfast

for

The Anthropological Association of Ireland

CONTENTS

Page

COMPARATIVE PERSPECTIVES

HISTORY, CULTURE, ETHNICITY

EDITORS' NOTES
AND ACKNOWLEDGEMENTS

With one exception the following essays are derived from papers and responses delivered at a conference entitled "Irish Travellers: History, Culture, Society", held in Dublin on 22nd-23rd February, 1991, and organised by the Anthropological Association of Ireland. Many of the contributions (including responses) have been considerably revised and expanded for publication. We have also included one paper – that by Thomas Acton – delivered in Dublin at an earlier conference organised by the Dublin Travellers' Education and Development Group. We are grateful to both Dr. Acton and the DTEDG for their willingness to include this paper, also revised, in the volume.

Because of some variation among contributors, we have standardised usage by introducing the upper case in all instances of the word "Traveller", while placing the adjective "travelling" in the lower case. Following a generally accepted precedent, we have used the lower case for the term "settled".

Séamas Ó Síocháin has co-ordinated the project since its inception and has played a crucial role in bringing it to fruition. His co-editors would like to acknowledge their appreciation of his investment of time and energy, and of his commitment.

The editors would like to express sincere thanks to a number of organisations, whose help made the original conference such a success: Co-operation North for vital financial assistance; the Dublin Travellers' Education and Development Group for advice and contact lists; Club na Múinteoirí for providing a congenial venue for the event; all the participants, who made it a very real encounter.

We wish to express our gratitude to the Cultural Traditions Group for a generous and necessary grant towards publication of the volume.

Helen Litton helped with indexing and general editorial work. Brian Walker and Kate Newmann of the Institute for Irish Studies provided encouragement and advice, when needed. Most particularly, we wish to thank the contributors, on whose work the whole project rests.

FOREWORD

This book continues a process which is exciting and
necessary for all of us. It challenges our assumptions and
undermines our pre-conceptions about one of the most
distinctive cultures on this island. The articles here cover a
wide area of interest, including valuable contributions from
members of the Traveller community. The references are
inclusive of many of the most complex questions which
concern a culture: history, origin, language and ethnicity.

The points made and the arguments raised here are eru-
dite and often fascinating. But their purpose will remain
incomplete if we fail to bring to them that single, vital act of
imagination which turns facts into faces and statistics into
human adventures. The story of the travelling people is our
story also. Too often, it has been a narrative of our anxiety
and resistance to difference. Yet in the relation between a
settled and a travelling community there are precious and
important possibilities for dialogue. It is a dialogue which
cannot happen unless perceptions shift and perceptions will
not shift until understanding replaces fear.

I was made particularly aware of this through the recent
architectural competition for designs for Travellers' accommodation. It was immediately clear – from the huge range
and excellence of the entries – that what had been elicited
were acts of insight as well as blueprints for living. You cannot
design the place in which a life occurs without having to
imagine that life also. In the process of imagining the lives of
Travellers, these designs and plans added to that slow growth
in perception which has been happening over the past few

years. In acknowledging the heritage of the Travellers and their housing needs these architectural statements – like the articles in this book – did far more than see the lives of Travellers as simply being different from those in the settled community. They also celebrated their distinctiveness and their persistent self-definition.

This book deserves a wide readership. Martin Collins, himself a Traveller, makes the comment in his article here that "we see ourselves as a distinct ethnic group". The issues of distinction and self-perception are vital to the understanding of the travelling people: their culture, their history, their value. But we need to be candid and see that those recognitions involve, first and foremost, our self-recognition as a settled society and our failures of understanding within it. And inasmuch as this book invites us to a partnership in acts of perception, imagination, and even self-accusation, I wholeheartedly welcome it.

Mary Robinson
Uachtarán na hÉireann

INTRODUCTION

Séamas Ó Síocháin, Joseph Ruane and May McCann

In the past 20 years majority groups in Ireland, North and South, have had to accept that the communities in which they live are far from homogeneous. Minorities exist – whether religious, political, cultural or sexual – with rights which must be recognised. The minorities in question have long been disadvantaged, but until recently were slow to assert their rights. This has changed and minority rights are now a central political issue. The disadvantages vary from group to group, but they might be summed up as the denial of the right to full participation in the society in which they live, the right to participate as different but as equal. Irish Travellers are one of these minorities.

There exists a small but rapidly growing research literature on Irish Traveller society and culture and on Traveller-settled community relations. It is a varied literature reflecting the disciplinary background of the researcher, the time in which it was carried out, the interests and concerns of the sponsors of the research, the assumptions made about the concepts, theories and methods appropriate to its subject. Like many other research areas, it is marked by controversy. Concepts and theories once widely used and accepted as self-evident are now strongly contested; some are rejected altogether. New concepts are revolutionising the field.

One of these concepts is ethnicity (see below). The concept has radical implications for the study of Irish Travellers because it approaches Traveller culture as distinct and valuable in its own right with its own historical path of development, rather than as a short-term adaptation to poverty or marginality. The concept has led to a new understanding of

Irish Travellers, their culture, and the policies appropriate to resolving conflicts between them and the settled community. It has identified the need for policies which respect cultural differences, rather than ones which seek to erode them in the name of the settled community's image of 'social improvement' or its administrative convenience.

The concept of ethnicity has already entered the public domain. There is disagreement, however, as to what it means and what it implies for policy making. The present volume grows out of a conference organised by the Anthropological Association of Ireland. The purpose of the conference was to provide a context in which new approaches to understanding Irish Travellers could be critically examined by academic researchers, Travellers, policy makers and the general public. The concept of ethnicity was at the heart of the matters discussed at the conference, although the issues raised go beyond it. The purpose of the book is to bring the contributions and debates to a wider audience. This introduction will first outline three theoretical and methodological principles that underlay the organisation of the conference and the selection of papers, before then looking at the issues raised.

One principle informing the organisation of the conference was the importance of comparison. A number of papers look at Irish Travellers in relation to Traveller and Gypsy groups in other European countries. Judith Okely looks at Traveller communities in Ireland, Scotland, Wales and England and in relation to the evolution of wide cultural and political relationships within and between the two islands, while Donald Kenrick offers a broad panoramic view of different groups in other parts of Europe. Sinéad Ní Shúinéar and Alice Binchy draw attention to research in the United States on the descendants of Irish Travellers who emigrated there more than 150 years ago. The volume also offers a comparative perspective on approaches used in the study of Traveller communities. Thus, Thomas Acton classifies approaches in terms of the assumptions they make about the origins of Traveller groups, the biological and/or cultural factors underlying their persistence as groups, and the policy implications that follow.

A second organising principle of the conference was the importance of history and of change over time. Ideally, we would have liked to include a paper by a historian drawing on all available historical sources to reconstruct the history of Travellers in Ireland. Unfortunately, that history has yet to be written; even the relevant sources have yet to be identified. Ní Shúinéar identifies some of the issues which will arise in writing this history and offers some general hypotheses that might guide research. No more is possible at the present time. However, it should be borne in mind that the subjective component of ethnicity means that the claim to ethnic separateness rests primarily on contemporary culture and identity, not on historical origins. It is not therefore a question of historical "fact" to be resolved by historical investigation. The crucial question is how Irish Travellers understand their experience at the present time.

The third organising principle was the importance of dialogue and debate. Provision was made for critical responses to many of the papers at the conference. But differences in approach, perspective and conclusion emerged even when a formal response was not explicitly provided for. This is due in large measure to the wide range of groups who attended the conference – Travellers, academic researchers, policy makers, social service professionals, advocates and others. In consequence, the volume should not be read as the elaboration of just one perspective on Irish Travellers – that of ethnicity – but as a critical dialogue involving many perspectives.

We look now in closer detail at some of the major themes addressed by the contributors to the volume.

ETHNICITY

The widespread use of the concept of ethnicity is the clearest example of new thinking in relation to Irish Travellers. The concept is systematically applied to the case of Irish Travellers by two of the contributors to the present volume (Ní Shúinéar and O'Connell), but it permeates the thinking of most contributors. In the process, a number of issues are thrown up, two of which merit individual comment: (i) the applicability of the term "ethnic group" to Irish Travellers, and (ii) the question of origins.

(i) Ní Shúinéar takes a standard anthropological definition (that of R. Narroll, as found in Barth, 1970) containing a number of criteria, which, when met, are claimed to identify a group as "ethnic". She applies these criteria to Irish Travellers and concludes that "we are dealing then with a group that fulfills all the objective criteria to qualify as an ethnic group" (p.60). O'Connell draws on a wider social science literature to point to some of the salient dimensions of ethnicity (its sociocultural character, involuntary membership, boundary maintenance). He then discusses Travellers as an ethnic group, assuming that the reader will accept the applicability of these dimensions to Irish Travellers. While Ní Shúinéar concentrates on objective characteristics, O'Connell stresses the subjective element and the fluidity of ethnicity ("ethnicity is something which is produced in historically specific contexts and it emerges, changes and adapts in meaning over time" p.111–2).

McLoughlin's is the only voice in the book which directly challenges the use of the term ethnicity in relation to Irish Travellers. This she does, firstly, by examining critically the criteria for ethnicity used by Ní Shúinéar and challenging the latter's interpretation of them. Secondly, she argues that to base a campaign for human rights on the special claim to ethnicity is to betray a conservative agenda (p.79). Better by far to recognise that society in the Republic of Ireland has been oppressively monolithic and that many minority groups have been denied full expression of their individuality (p.85ff.). Travellers would be better to view themselves as one minority among others and join in the broader fight for a more pluralist society.

McLoughlin is not alone, however, in identifying and criticising ideologies and regimes of "homogeneity and conformity" (p.86). O'Connell does likewise (p.114f.) in the Irish context, while Okely ("There is not – and cannot be a single, monolithic way of living in Europe . . ." p.1) and Acton do so in a broader, European, context. They differ, however, in their assessment of what role the ethnic claim should play in working towards a more pluralist, less oppressive, society. In part, the issue comes down to one of definition: are Irish Travellers an ethnic group, a culture or a sub-culture? McLoughlin accepts that Travellers are "a distinct group within Irish society" (p.91) but disputes the claim to ethnicity, while O'Connell and most other contributors view them as an ethnic group with a distinct culture (see "Traveller Culture" below).

(ii) A second dimension of the ethnicity question is that of origins: if Irish Travellers are an ethnic group, when did they become so? Contributors differ over whether the question of origins should be put at all (see "Comparative Perspective" below) and, if it is, over the likely date for the emergence of Irish Travellers as an ethnic group.

Until recently, conventional wisdom held that Travellers derived from the Irish peasantry, from people dispossessed of their land and forced onto the roads from the time of Cromwell to the Irish famine (Ní Shúinéar summarises this view, p. 66). A distinct ethnic identity emerged gradually over time. This is the viewpoint offered, for example, by Sharon and George Gmelch, the first to formulate an argument for Traveller ethnicity (1976). None of the contributors to the present volume seems to find this periodisation acceptable. Ní Shúinéar hypothesises that Traveller origins should be sought in the early Irish historical period, either from a pre-Celtic group, from one of a number of Celtic groups, or from indigenous itinerant craftworkers of the early Christian period (p.70ff.). This is linked to her view of Gammon (the Traveller language) as very ancient and as underlying Traveller use of English. Travellers have maintained their ethnic separateness from the surrounding Irish society throughout the centuries, partly through language, through endogamy (marriage within the group), and through broader cultural differences.

In contrast, it could be inferred from Binchy's essay that she sees Traveller ethnicity as emerging at the present time. She introduces a Four Stage dynamic model which places groups on a continuum from acquiescence in their disadvantaged position (Stage One) to a point (Stage Four) of challenge to the status quo and claim to ethnic separateness. Some Travellers are now at Stage Three of this continuum, unwilling to assimilate, protesting against the injustices of the system and seeking to mobilise support for a positive social identity (p.141ff). Kenny refers to the emergent consciousness of nations, including that of Ireland at the beginning of the twentieth century, and views ethnic groups also as emergent phenomena. Her statement that "in the early days of the Travellers' emergence as a people they were 'spoken for' . . ." (p.183), implies the recent acquisition of that status.

Finally, while not devoting great detail to the history of Irish Travellers, Acton implies that some Romany Gypsies reached Ireland in the sixteenth century, to be absorbed by an existing Irish Traveller Community (p.48).

TRAVELLER CULTURE

Closely related to the claim to ethnic status is the question of Traveller culture. For many contributors the analytical starting-point here is the rejection of the "culture of poverty" approach. As Patricia McCarthy points out, this theory was formulated by the anthropologist, Oscar Lewis, based on a series of studies of the urban poor in Mexico. It sought to account for the persistence of urban poverty by attributing it (at least partly) to a culture which evolved among the poor, which was passed down from generation to generation and which was extremely difficult to break down. In her 1972 thesis Patricia McCarthy analysed Irish Travellers as a "culture of poverty". Within the social sciences the theory was subsequently subjected to strenuous criticism and Patricia McCarthy now views it as untenable.

"Culture of poverty" theory has been criticised for ignoring the structural causes of poverty, i.e. the unbalanced power relations in society, which keep various sectors of society, (the urban poor, but also peasants, women and ethnic minorities) bound in a situation of continued deprivation. Its application to Irish Travellers has been criticised on similar grounds (see "Traveller-Settled Community Relations" below). However, it has also been rejected for assuming that Travellers are members of a "sub-culture" rather than a culture in its own right. McCarthy's essay in this volume argues the case. Ní Shúinéar's reference to Traveller's "fundamental cultural values" also assumes that they form a culture, rather than a sub-culture.

These values include nomadism, which we look at separately. They also include the patriarchal and extended family, independence and flexibility in economic adaptation, a resistance to wage labour in favour of self-employment, rituals surrounding death, and rituals of cleansing. These cultural elements are itemised by a range of contributors (Okely, Ní Shúinéar and McCarthy in particular), although, unfortunately, without in-depth ethnographic description. However, the comparative perspective introduced by Okely and Kenrick is important here. Okely points out that most of these characteristics are shared by English, Welsh, Scottish and Irish Travellers (p.8f.). Kenrick, having presented a welcome survey of other travelling groups in Europe, states that "there is no common deep culture shared by all the nomads of Europe or even by all the non-Romany groups" (p.28). But he allows some shared cultural characteristics, probably based on the necessity of travelling rather than on "a common origin and common set of beliefs" (*ibid*).

NOMADISM

Nomadism is an important topic in the contributions to this volume. Kenny describes it as "the core value of Traveller culture", identifying it as "not necessarily the intention to keep travelling, but the nomadic mindset" (p.180). Okely distinguishes the nomadism of Travellers from that of the classical hunter-gatherers and pastoral nomads described by anthropologists, in that Traveller society is closely interknit with the wider sedentary society (p.4f). Acton describes it as economic or commercial nomadism (e.g. p.37). While, in the past, tin-kering was a common economic activity, as is

scrap-dealing today, all the authors strongly reject the identification of Travellers with any specific occupation. They value,
above all, self-employment (McDonagh p.98) and flexibility in
identifying "gaps in the dominant system of supply and demand" (Okely p.5) and the range of services Travellers offer is
very wide (see the interesting list given by Ní Shúinéar p.64f).

*In addition to its economic function nomadism also serves
important psychological, social and cultural functions.
McDonagh suggests that the nomadic mind-set permeates
every aspect of Travellers' lives. "Nomadism entails a way of
looking at the world, a different way of perceiving things, a
different attitude to accommodation, to work, and to life in
general"(p.95). Moving into a house, for example, followed
by the growing realization that they may have to remain there
permanently, can be a "terrifying experience" (*ibid*).

Nomadism serves the social function of allowing small
family groups, which normally travel together, to meet a
wider range of kin so that news is shared and young people
can come into contact with a wide range of potential marriage partners (McDonagh p.97). In contrast, when relations
become strained, moving away becomes a mechanism for
avoiding social tension. Attitudes to death and sexual morality are also affected by nomadism (Binchy p.150).

The importance of nomadism expresses itself in material
culture. Trailers and vans are important symbolically and
financially. As McCarthy points out, "Travellers spend their
money on what they can take with them when travelling and
therefore a very significant percent of their expenditure is on
transport – cars and vans and specifically on the kind of
transport that enables them to earn a living" (p.126). Jewellery is also important: "Travellers carry their wealth by wearing it" (McDonagh p.99).

Nomadism has also affected Traveller language. Speaking
of Gammon or Shelta, Binchy hypothesises that Traveller
language developed as it did because of nomadism (see
"Language" below). Kenny suggests that nomadism also affects Traveller use of English; for example, the habitual use
of the verb "to go *on*", where we would say "to go", reveals a
Traveller mind-set (p.184).

Ironically, as Kenny points out, this core value of Traveller life has been "turned ... into a key instrument of their oppression, ensuring that forced movement is the only experience of nomadism most Travellers have" (p.180). A great deal of Michael McDonagh's discussion of "the real world" centres on the specifics of this oppression: prohibition orders, inferior accommodation, and the use of boulders, mounds of clay, rubble and deep trenches to hinder Traveller mobility (p.104ff.).

LANGUAGE

Most of the contributors refer to Traveller language in some context, but two are devoted specifically to the topic (Binchy and Ó Baoill). They make substantial contributions to what is, sadly, a neglected topic. The focus of both is on Gammon or Cant (Shelta – a non-Traveller term – is used by Binchy), with passing reference to Traveller use of Hiberno or Irish English.

Binchy outlines how, at the end of the last century, academic members of the settled community in England became aware of the existence of Gammon. It became the object of folkloristic and linguistic studies, opinions differing as to whether it was an ancient or relatively modern language. She deals also with another old debate – whether Gammon is a "secret" language – and examines it in the context of Travellers as a marginal, oppressed, group, similar to refugees or emigrants. She argues that Gammon is a crucial "ethnic marker" for Travellers, including for a community of American Travellers, descendants of Irish Travellers who migrated to the United States at the time of the Famine. It is in this context that she draws on the Four Stage dynamic model on linguistic strategies adopted in intergroup relations, in order to locate Travellers on a continuum of growing group awareness. Stage Three, where she places some Travellers, involves efforts to achieve "a more positive social identity", with emphasis on the "ethnic language" (p.141ff).

Both Binchy and Ó Baoill try to place Gammon in relation to classifications current among linguists. Pidgins, creoles and social registers are discussed, though it emerges that none fits exactly. "Its grammar and syntactic structure is overwhelmingly English...", writes Ó Baoill, "but a substantial part of its vocabulary and idioms are unrecognisable as anything remotely English." It is used for communication *within* a definite group and from the cradle. Clearly, Gammon's failure to develop a grammar of its own is a major puzzle for the linguist. Binchy suggests the effect of nomadism:

> *"The social setting of Shelta is small family groups, nomadic islands in a sedentary sea, signalling to each other across that sea, and united by the collection of habits and dispositions that we call Traveller culture. The hypothesis is that the dispersion caused by nomadic habits has caused the language to develop as it has. In the present system, lexicon is the ethnic marker, and grammar represents the part of life shared with settled society." (p.150)*

Ó Baoill addresses a number of other crucial issues. The first is the period of origin of Gammon. His conclusion is that "the Cant must have been created at a time when its original speakers were bilingual, having a knowledge of both Irish and English. This would seem to date the creation as sometime in the last 350 years or so" (p.160).

A second issue for Ó Baoill is why Gammon appears to have fossilized, i.e. is not now generating new words and idioms. Not only are new words not being generated, the existing store seems to be declining. However, the reader gets conflicting signals on this from different contributors. Binchy writes that "the range of Shelta lexicon, as well as direct fieldwork evidence, are indicators that Shelta has a wider usage than was previously thought" (p.137). For McCarthy: "Travellers' language, Cant or Gammon, is still widely understood but not widely used anymore. My impression is that a fairly restricted number of words and phrases is still in common usage" (p.126). Ní Shúinéar cites Harper's opinion that the average Gammon vocabulary of Georgia Travellers aged 35 and over was 150 words, and half that for the younger generation (p.65f). Ó Baoill believes the same to be true of Irish Travellers.

This brings him to a third issue, that of the future of Gammon. He writes:

"In conclusion, may I add that what is really important now is not the origin of Cant, whatever it may be, but its FUTURE. In this respect Travellers themselves must decide how they want it developed, cultivated, taught in schools and extended in away that will make it an integral part of their own self-identity in every sphere of their daily lives" (p.168).

He includes in his essay some concrete suggestions for research into Traveller language, aimed at strengthening its role in relation to Traveller identity.

Closely related to the discussion of Gammon is that of Travellers' use of English, especially Irish English or Hiberno English. Ó Baoill introduces the topic with a series of questions:

"Do Travellers use different varieties of English in their everyday communication, and if they do, how do they (these varieties) interact and, more importantly, what are the social functions that are attached to each variety? Where then does Traveller's Cant fit into the scheme of things? When the Cant is avoided what takes its place – general Irish English, non-standard Irish English, standard English? We know very little about such matters at the present time" (p.162).

Binchy suggests that Travellers, like emigrants, learn only enough of the language of the host society (English in the case of Travellers) to make themselves understood. Gammon is reserved for intra-group communication, where it fulfils the integrative, expressive and directive functions of language as opposed to the propositional or referential.

Two final points on language. The first is the extent, if any, of Romani words in Traveller language. The possibility is mentioned by Acton (pp. 38–9) but not discussed in the papers devoted specifically to language. The second is to draw attention, as Kenny does, to the existence of ethnocentric usages in the language used by settled people. Indeed, she prefers the term "sedentary" over "settled" because of the loaded value content of the latter.

COMPARATIVE PERSPECTIVE

Two of the contributors, Okely and Acton, make a special plea for a comparative approach to the topic of Irish Travellers, though from different points of view. Okely focuses on the ethnocentric labellings made by members of the dominant society, especially the classification of travelling people into romantically-conceived exotic Romanies, on the one hand, and "drop-out" Tinkers, on the other. This type of labelling, she argues, tells us more about the biases of the dominant society than it does about historical realities. The process of labelling and its significance might not be adverted to if one were to focus exclusively on Irish Travellers. It can only be recognised for what it is by seeing its contrasting application to "Romany" Gypsies and to Irish, English, Scottish and Welsh "tinkers". In her repudiation of the quest for Indian origins and racial purity, Okely tends to stress characteristics which all Traveller-Gypsies share (p.8f) and she comes close to rejecting a historical approach as well as a focus on cultural differences between different groups of Traveller-Gypsies.

Acton's plea for a comparative approach rests on a different argument. He argues that an over-focus on local identities diverts attention away from the shared fate of European Gypsy-Travellers historically – to our peril. His thesis is that there was an influx of Gypsy-Travellers from India at an identifiable period in European history; that a trans-European commercial nomadism flourished for some time subsequently, in which Irish Travellers participated; and that a major genocide of Gypsy-Travellers took place, connected with the emergence of agricultural capitalism and the nation-state (the late Tudor period in England). During this period vagrants and foreigners became prime targets, and Gypsies were both. In response, Gypsy-Travellers could only survive by becoming localized, taking on local identities and patrons, within the new political units. Today, we need to undergo the cathartic exercise of admitting the 16th century holocaust, in order to help divest ourselves of our racist myths. An exclusive focus on local Traveller identities hinders this process.

Kenrick's paper gives the reader detailed pen-sketches of the range of groups in mainland Europe who are similar to Irish Travellers. He is more comfortable with the Romany/non-Romany distinction than is Okely. His survey covers different national groups (Jenisch, Mercheros, Reisende etc.) and contrasting cultural practices associated, for example, with death, marriage and language. Where cultural characteristics are common to different groups (e.g. "the extreme attention to cleanliness of food and clothing"), he suggests that this is "more likely due to the necessity for this when travelling, than to a common origin and common set of beliefs" (p.28). Because of their shared nomadism, he believes that "in their way of life Irish Travellers are closer to nomadic Romany groups than the latter are to sedentary Romany groups"(p.30).

TRAVELLER-SETTLED COMMUNITY RELATIONS

Another change in perspective illustrated in this volume relates to Traveller-settled community relationships. At one time those in the settled community concerned with Traveller issues viewed Travellers as a poverty-group in need of help towards assimilation. Binchy (p.143) illustrates this well: "The original Itinerant Settlement Commission, set up in the early 1960s [had].. the avowed aim of assimilating Travellers into the settled community: 'it is not considered that there is any alternative to a positive drive for housing itinerants, if a permanent solution to the problem of itinerancy, based on absorption and integration, is to be achieved.'" (Report of the Commission on Itinerancy, 1963 p.62). The newer approach, focuses on Traveller culture and identity, appeals for justice rather than charity, and charges the dominant settled community with bias and discrimination.

Okely, for example, begins her essay with the anthropological concept of ethnocentrism, "the tendency to judge and value everyone else's way of life by one's own" (p.1). She refers to the growing practice among anthropologists of "study-ing up", i.e. looking at the "dominant power structures" operating in society (p.2). She discusses the topic of Travel-ler-Gypsies in Great Britain and Ireland using the concept of "internal colonialism".

"My intention is to demonstrate that the perception of Irish Travel-lers even within Ireland needs to be examined in a context beyond its shores. The ways in which Irish, Scottish, Welsh or English Travellers are labelled are part of an interlocking pattern and linked to internal colonialism" (pp.3-4).

She argues that various theories of Traveller or Gypsy origin have much more to do with the needs of settled community theorists than with historical fact. For example, the suggestion that there are genuine pure-blooded Gypsies, of Indian origin, as opposed to unauthentic drop-outs, Tinkers etc. is a reflec-tion of the dominant society's need to project its longings onto 'other' imaginary peoples (p.6). And:

"The question arises why local origins have been seen as positive in the Irish and Scottish cases, but not in the English and Welsh cases? The answer lies in the historical circumstances of internal colonial-ism" (p.14).

There is also cause for reflection in Kenny's observation that, even in the conference from which the present volume de-rives, "the agenda of the sedentary dominated" (p.181). On the other hand, one of the hopeful signs of recent years has been the strengthening of the Traveller voice and of Travel-ler action, as evidenced by the emergence of the Irish Travel-ler Movement (McDonagh p.108). Kenny lists other develop-ments, such as Traveller pilgrimages, radio programmes, and the national Traveller Women's Forum (p.187).

POLICY

Many of the contributors criticise current government policies as deriving from an assimilationist or "Traveller-as-problem" viewpoint. In contrast, the policies they advocate derive from their acceptance of the Traveller way of life as a distinct and valuable cultural alternative. Noonan, for example, criticises the Northern Ireland Department of the Environment's "Toleration Policy" (p.172) as well as the guiding viewpoint of the Government Report on Travelling People (p.174). Both reflect the unwillingness of officialdom to take Traveller ethnic status seriously (p.170). On the other hand, positive precedents are to be found in provisions of the Standing Advisory Committee on Human Rights, which does take the issue of ethnicity seriously (p.175ff.).

Collins suggests that a submerged theoretical approach – akin to the "(sub-)culture of poverty theory" – guides the actions of officials, even when they do not consciously recognise the fact. "They sometimes admit that they do not recognise Travellers as having a distinct cultural identity". This is implicit in the refusal of officials to recognise economically successful Travellers as Travellers, since they are not poor by definition (McDonagh p.106). The consequence of a policy that aims to "help" Travellers to "integrate" into the "community", says McDonagh, is that: "the system makes people dependent on it, taking pride and independence away with one hand and giving the dole and second-hand clothes with the other" (p.107).

The implications are clearly spelt out by Kenny:

"Our difficulty with Traveller economy and accommodation is linked to failure to legitimise nomadism itself: this is evident in the chronic failure to take commercial nomadism as an economic way of life into account in the location of sites. In order to understand and act appropriately, we need to listen to Travellers, but this includes recognising the silencing of their traditions which their delegitimation has imposed: as an integral part of listening we must allow them opportunities to undo internal and internalised colonialism, we must return to them the space to come to terms with their experience and to find their voice" (p.185).

CONCLUSION

Substantial areas of agreement may be found in the contributions to this volume. The most notable agreement is on the need to recognise Travellers as a distinct cultural minority, with all the practical consequences of such recognition for the dominant settled community, including policy makers. But there is also disagreement: on the relevance of the ethnic claim to minority rights, on the history of Traveller language and the emergence of Travellers as a distinct group, on the pertinence of historical questions as such, on the linguistic nature and extent of usage of Gammon or Shelta.

Whatever one's position on these disputed issues, they point to the need for further ethnographic, historical and linguistic research. But, as pointed out earlier, the subjective nature of ethnicity means that the claim to ethnic distinctiveness (or to human and civic rights) is not something to be denied until "validated" by such research. Finally, it is hoped that the present volume will highlight the need both for further research and for the recognition of the Traveller lifestyle as a distinct and valuable cultural alternative in its own right.

REFERENCES

Barth, F. *Ethnic Groups and Boundaries*. London: Allen & Unwin, 1970.

Commission on Itinerancy *Report of the Commission on Itinerancy*. Dublin: Stationery Office, 1963.

Gmelch, G. and S.B. Gmelch "The Emergence of an Ethnic Group: The Irish Tinkers", *Anthropological Quarterly*, 49 (4), 1976, 225-38.

McCarthy, P. *Itinerancy and Poverty: a Study in the Sub-Culture of Poverty*. Unpublished M.Soc.Sc. Thesis. Dublin: University College, 1972.

AN ANTHROPOLOGICAL PERSPECTIVE ON IRISH TRAVELLERS

Judith Okely

Social anthropology looks at the full range of human socie-ties and culture and takes seriously the understanding and study of alternative ways of life. It confronts what has come to be called ethnocentrism, i.e. the tendency to judge and value everyone else's way of life by one's own. It also examines and often critically deconstructs what is *assumed* to be the norm, the ideal and the only rational way of being.

Anthropology doesn't just look at exotic, distant lands, but also at the West, and at Europe. It is concerned with the full range of Europeans, including Travellers, and with other ways of being European, other ways of being Irish or British. The Travellers or Gypsies are just one example of this wide range. There is not – and cannot be – a single, monolithic way of living in Europe, let alone elsewhere. So often policy makers and politicians with power are under the illusion there is a single way of doing things and come unstuck when confronted with regional or sectarian interests. They also come unstuck when faced with minority groups like the Travellers. The Travellers have little or no opportunity to voice their point of view. They are not a powerful voting lobby. The planners and politicians are far more likely to hear and listen to the anti-Traveller lobby, especially since housedwellers have greater power through the ballot box and because their way of life seems more akin to that of the decision makers.

In the traditions of social anthropology in which I have been taught, social anthropologists have lived alongside the people they want to learn about. They listen to what the people say, believe and think. Anthropologists want to know how people structure their world. In so far as it is possible, they look at people's experience from the inside, although of course the anthropologist cannot easily become a fully paid up member of the group. It happens also that the anthropologist may choose to study his or her own original group. I have done both in my time. I lived for two years with Travellers in England and kept in touch with them for a decade, while also visiting or staying with Gypsies or Travellers in Ireland, France, Sweden and the Netherlands. My study also included policy makers' and housedwellers' beliefs and treatment of Travellers (Okely 1975, 1983). I have also studied people from my own group, e.g. members of my former girls' boarding school (Okely 1978).

It should not be thought that anthropologists only select the exotic, the minority, the 'other' when choosing to study, even within Europe. Increasingly, anthropologists engage in what has been called "studying up" i.e. they look at the dominant power structures, and they also focus on the beliefs and experience of ostensibly majority populations. Studying the wider context of the dominant or majority society is crucial when focussing on a minority group, for the latter's experience and beliefs are always in part formed by the need to respond to the dominant society. So when presenting an anthropological perspective on Travellers, I should include: first, the inside views and experience of the Travellers themselves; second, the views and experience of non-Travellers – both powerful decision makers and the mass of housedwellers, with particular emphasis on their attitudes to and relations with Travellers; third, the total context of Traveller – non-Traveller relations, whose aspects change according to economic circumstances, national or international political pressures and prevailing ideologies.

My presentation draws on first-hand experience of Irish Travellers mainly in England but with some encounters in Ireland. I have also examined some of the writings *about* Irish Travellers. My sources include the work of social scientists, historians, folklorists and the writings of non-academics in local and national government reports and newspapers. My first-hand empirical comments are based on extensive fieldwork and experience with Travellers or Gypsies in England, whether Irish, Scottish, Welsh or English, as well as those from the continental mainland. This experience will help to throw light on many of the misunderstandings to which Travellers have been subjected in Ireland.

When we look at the history of Gypsies or Travellers in Europe we find dramatic changes in their treatment and experiences. During the Second World War they were rounded up on the Continent by the Nazis and many perished in concentration camps and gas chambers. Too often the Holocaust is depicted as something which Jews alone suffered, and it has been extremely difficult for Gypsy survivors to obtain reparations. During the war, Ireland as a neutral country experienced the migration of British born Gypsies who did not wish to join the army. Other British Gypsies were recruited into the forces and some were present at the liberation of Belsen.

The post-war period saw further changes, with different implications for the Travellers. Many Irish Travellers, along with their compatriots, migrated to Britain in search of economic opportunities. At a time when there was extensive demand by housedwellers for the Travellers' type of work, the British government introduced legislation which restricted the possibilities for Travellers to camp legally on land – whether as temporary stopping places or for long-term residence – on which they had once paid rent and rates. The consent of the land owner became irrelevant. All these differing contexts affect both how the Travellers are perceived by non-Travellers and how they respond to them.

During the 1960s in Britain the Gypsies or Travellers became more visible on roadsides. It was then that the anti-Gypsy lobby tended to label many if not all Travellers as not "real" Gypsies but Tinkers. They were often labelled Irish and linked with the most pejorative and racist stereotypes.

You may wonder why I've shifted to talking about England. My intention is to demonstrate that the perception of Irish Travellers even within Ireland needs to be examined in a context beyond its shores. The ways in which Irish, Scottish,

Welsh or English Travellers are labelled are part of an interlocking pattern and linked to internal colonialism. I was able to meet, get to know and live near many Irish Travellers in England during my fieldwork. Some had been born in England, had never been to Ireland, but classified themselves as Irish, spoke with Irish or gammon accents, and were so identified by both English Travellers and housedwellers. The housedwellers, however, often did not distinguish between Irish Travellers and Irish housedwelling migrants. If there was an anti-Irish feeling in the area or in the prevailing political climate, all Irish suffered, whatever their own self-identities. There were other examples of Irish Travellers having married English Travellers. If the former no longer travelled to Ireland, their offspring or descendants could pass as English Romany.

Pivotal to my presentation is the relationship between Travellers and non- Travellers. By the latter I mean members of the dominant housedwelling society. Throughout Europe and in North America Travellers refer to non-Travellers by the term "gajé" or "gorgio". The label is pejorative. A gorgio – and I am one – is usually seen as polluted, stupid and potentially persecuting. The Scottish Travellers call non-Travellers "flatties" – i.e. people who live in flats. In Scotland much urban residential housing consists of flats rather than self-contained houses. The Irish Travellers use, among other labels, "country people" or "buffers". This may reflect the once predominantly rural population of Irish housedwellers in the past. In the middle of urban Watford, just north of London, I have heard Irish Travellers refer to non-Travellers as country people. The labels which Travellers adopt for themselves will in part be affected by the labels given them by gorgios, flatties or country people.

Travellers do not and cannot live, work and survive in a vacuum. Gypsies, Tsiganes, Tinkers or Travellers are a unique group around the world. They do not fall into the classical anthropological typology of nomads, for they are interdependent with a wider sedentary economy. They do not live in the wild off natural produce as hunter-gatherer nomads, nor do they depend mainly on animal herds as do pastoral nomads. As I have extensively outlined elsewhere (Okely 1975, 1983) they provide occasional goods and services where there are gaps in the dominant system of supply and demand. They must follow the shifts in the wider economy and make the necessary adaptation. Studies from Asia to Eastern and Western Europe and the Americas have documented their remarkable flexibility. They are not parasitic for, if given geographical mobility and legal residence, temporary or permanent, in suitable areas of work, they make a significant contribution to the economy. These aspects are invariably overlooked by outsiders, who either forget or fail to notice individual economic transactions between Traveller and non-Traveller.

Throughout the history of Traveller – non-Traveller relationships we find a variety of responses by the majority non-Traveller society. Travellers or Gypsies have sometimes been accepted and tolerated as vaguely different. At other times the difference has not been tolerated and attempts have been made to control Travellers or to change them. When that policy has failed or when the level of intolerance of difference became extreme, policies have been instigated to destroy Travellers either through enforced assimilation or tragically by genocide. At other times the difference between Travellers and non-Travellers has been exaggerated and mythologised. Travellers or Gypsies have been accredited with exotic, romantic qualities. This exoticisation might appear harmless and aesthetically enriching when found in poetry, painting, opera and fiction, but the imagery lives on and may be used as a device to reject most if not all living Travellers and Gypsies. Once perceived as exotic beings, the circumstances are ripe for dividing dream from reality, phantom from person.

Let us examine how this has worked in relation to Irish Travellers. The very nomenclature is interpreted as meaning that Irish Travellers are *not* Gypsies. Travellers associated with Ireland, as well as Scotland were previously called Tinkers. In fact I found that the Gypsies associated with both England and Wales often use the label Traveller in preference to the pejorative history attributed to the label Gypsy.

That is why I called my book *The Traveller-Gypsies*. We do not find Travellers linked to Ireland or Scotland calling themselves Gypsies unless they claim some connection with English (or Welsh) Travellers/Gypsies. Here there seems to be an agreement between both Travellers and non-Travellers. It appears to be part of the ideology of both the minority group and the dominant sedentary society, whether in Ireland or Britain, that Gypsies are *not* Irish. This has serious implications for the Irish Travellers whenever "Gypsy" is seen as a positive, exotic label. Gypsies have been associated with powerful cultural characters – e.g. Bizet's Carmen. In Ireland Travellers may be labelled as not Gypsies and appear therefore less authentic as a distinct culture.

A divisive process also occurs in Britain where there are said to be "real" Gypsies and "counterfeit" ones. The counterfeits are dismissed as drop-outs from the dominant society. By contrast the real ones are allegedly of a distinct "race"; originating from abroad, allegedly India, on the basis of linguistic links. Ideally the so-called "pure blooded" ones are self- sufficient, good mannered and isolated in rural enclaves. All this is of course fantasy and tells us more about the dominant society's need to project its longings onto "other" imaginary peoples. The Gypsies or Travellers working with scrap metal near urban areas are dismissed as drop-outs, since it is held that the real ones are extinct. This stereotyping process is familiar both to Travellers and to those closely acquainted with them.

Sociologists, historians, anthropologists in Britain and in the rest of Europe have been writing about and contesting for decades the divisive stereotypes. It is all the more unnerving that these arguments have to be rehearsed yet again. As Sinéad Ní Shúinéar suggests (see Chapter 4), the question of Travellers' origins comes up repeatedly, and less for academic reasons than for political reasons (personal communication and this volume). In prevailing political circumstances in order to claim greater self-determination and freedom from enforced assimilation or persecution, Travellers or Gypsies may seek recognition from the dominant society as a cultural or ethnic minority with specific rights. The labels which are given to them and those which they give themselves both reflect and reinforce their current political position.

Elsewhere (Okely 1983) I have indicated scepticism as to the exotic foreign origin of even persons called "real" Gypsies in Britain either today or in the past. Language moves and changes separately from groups of people. Whether one likes it or not, the prevailing language in Ireland is English. But this does *not* mean that the Irish are descended from the English! Language gives us clues to some past relationships – e.g. colonial conquest or trade.

The word Gypsy derives from "Egyptian". Yet no one now suggests that Gypsies migrated from Egypt in the fifteenth or sixteenth century when the label appeared. The Travellers' or Gypsies' history is defined and fixed by the written sources and records of non-Gypsies. A category of persons called "Egyptians" was first recorded in the British Isles in 1505, in the accounts of the Lord High Treasurer in Scotland. They presented themselves to James IV as pilgrims, their leader being lord of "Little Egypt" (Vesey-Fitzgerald 1973, 21). This category of persons was first recorded in England in 1514; an "Egyptian" woman who could "tell marvellous things by look-ing into one's hands" (Vesey-Fitzgerald 1973, 28). It is not clear whether Egyptian was taken to mean a person from Egypt or just a foreigner or stranger. Both in the British Isles and elsewhere in Europe, well before Gypsies or "Tsiganes" were publicly recorded in western Europe (in the fourteenth century), "All mountebanks and travelling showmen found themselves dubbed 'Egyptians'" (Clébert 1967, 27) Persons believed by many Gypsiologists to be the first Gypsies arriving in western Europe presented themselves as pilgrims, some from "Little Egypt" understood to represent the Middle East (Vesey-Fitzgerald 1973, 13; Vaux de Foletier 1970, 20-l).

It is not at all clear whether these so-called foreign Egyp-tians ever came from abroad. In 1562 the death penalty was introduced for those *"calling themselves* Egyptians" (my empha-sis) and for those "counterfeiting, transforming or disguising themselves by their Apparel, Speech or other behaviour" (Thompson 1928). This suggests that the Egyptian title was nothing but an assumed identity for many persons with no foreign origin. It may have been a convenient means of self-identification among Gypsies in order to present an exotic identity as fortune tellers and dancers. Further evidence reveals a description of a hundred Gypsies in the early seventeenth century who went about "causing their face to be made blacke, as if they were Egyptians" (Thompson 1928, 34). Thus the popular view that all the early Gypsies were innately different in physiognomy or so called "racial origin" should be treated with scepticism.

It was not until the late 18th and early 19th centuries that scholars and linguists claimed an Indian origin for Gypsies, on the basis of various forms of Romany "language", dialects or vocabulary. In the folklorist and other literature the claim is that the "real" Gypsies are found in England and Wales but not in Ireland or Scotland. The fact that the first "Egyptian" was recorded in Scotland is strangely overlooked. Yet the presence of "Egyptians" in Scotland was not just a one-off record in 1505. Again in 1530 "Egyptians" danced for James V in Holyrood House, Edinburgh, and were rewarded for their entertainment.

I suggest that the sub-classification of Gypsies or Travellers in Britain and Ireland in terms of the presence or absence of exotic Indian Romany origins, has more to do with internal colonialism than with actual differences between the groups. Gypsies or Travellers are both defined and sub-classified by the dominant society and by themselves. There are many aspects of Gypsy or Traveller culture which the different groups have in common, it is only the labels, the territorial and kinship allegiances, and local contexts for working and living which demarcate differences.

What do the English or Welsh Gypsies and Irish or Scottish Travellers have in common? They share a resistance to wage-labour, a multiplicity of self-employed occupations, often a need for geographical flexibility and an ideological preference for trailers or caravans. Among all groups there are extremes of wealth or relative poverty, some may move into housing, some may "pass" into the dominant society, marry people outside the ethnic group and choose to take up wage-labour.

Among English, Scottish, Welsh and Irish Travellers membership is based on descent. A person has to have at least one Traveller or Gypsy parent to claim membership. The children of a mixed marriage between Traveller and gorgio/country person can claim rights of membership through descent. Whenever possible during fieldwork I recorded genealogical evidence among English and Irish Travellers. In all nationally labelled groups, they used the same principle. No one could simply take to the road and become a Traveller – he or she could gain some acceptance through marriage, but only the offspring could claim full ethnic identity. A detailed anthropological study of Scottish Travellers by Farnum Rehfisch (1958) alerted me to this principle which he first recorded among Scottish Travellers. In all groups I found some marriages with non-Travellers whose offspring were given full ethnic identity.

English, Scottish, Welsh and Irish Travellers also share pollution beliefs. Rehfisch recorded and expanded in personal communication to me the existence of pollution beliefs among Scottish Travellers. I found pollution beliefs among English, Irish and Welsh Travellers in Britain. There is also evidence of the same pollution beliefs among Travellers in Ireland. Unfortunately, earlier social scientists like George and Sharon Gmelch did not investigate such beliefs and practices among the Travellers whom they studied, dismissing them as "mere superstitions" or casual copying from English Gypsies. Informal conversations with George and Sharon Gmelch in the 1970s, and brief encounters with Travellers in Ireland, convinced me that these pollution beliefs existed. Later work by Sinéad Ní Shúinéar among Travellers in Ireland confirms the existence of such beliefs (personal communication and this volume.)

The example of pollution beliefs shows how the popular labelling of Irish Travellers as recent drop-outs without a distinct ethnic identity affected the perceptions of earlier social scientists. Sharon and George Gmelch did not see what Irish Travellers shared with so-called Gypsies. They were intent on testing and applying the American theory of a "culture of poverty". I come from a different anthropological b.s

tradition. They dismissed as "old fashioned" the anthropological approach which I described to them and which entails
listening to the Travellers without preconceived hypotheses,
without deciding in advance what focus was relevant.

The danger of imposing preconceived "theories" from the
start and filtering out all other information and knowledge is
that crucial material from the people themselves goes un-
heard, unrecorded. A commitment or addiction merely to
testing ready worked-out hypotheses means that the agenda
and questions are set in advance by the researcher. In the
case of Travellers and Gypsies, who are so vulnerable to
outsiders' labels and perceptions, the researcher risks treat-
ing those labels as objective facts which in turn affect what
the researcher looks for and claims to see.

A vivid example of the dangers of this approach comes
from a researcher from a department of anatomy at the
University of Oxford (Clarke 1973). There is a popular and
prevailing belief that Travellers in the four nationalities of
the British Isles (including Northern Ireland and The Republic of Ireland) are to be distinguished, not only by their
current choice of national allegiance or identity, but also by
each national subgroup's alleged place of origin – either
foreign or indigenous. The seemingly objective scientific
procedure of Dr Clarke, apparently a physical anthropologist, was entirely coloured by this prevailing social
classification. He set out to examine the ethnic origins of
Gypsies travelling in Britain in the late 1960's and collected
blood specimens from 250 Travellers in England. Significantly he chose that location – not Scotland, not Ireland.

Those individuals who agreed to the test were classified
into five groups according to a questionnaire asking about
family history, and according to their "physical appearance"
– despite the fact that external characteristics (the apparent
phenotype) have been discredited as a reliable guide to
people's genetic make up (genotype). Type A were "those
having some Romany lineage"; Types B to E were non-
Romany itinerants (including doubtful cases), classified
according to the four geographical origins – England, Scotland, Wales and Ireland (Clarke 1973, 187). Clarke took

indigenous origins for the Irish and Scottish Travellers as given. Indeed he chose only to report on the tests made on the 109 so-called "Romanies" identified by him and by their own self-presentation.

It is clear now – if it was not then – from the literature on Travellers, that the way Travellers choose to describe themselves to outsiders depends on who is asking the questions, what the context is and what the Travellers stand to gain or lose by the labels. Indeed two of the Scottish Travellers encountered by Clarke and living in Essex who were married to English Travellers came up with an explanation for their travelling origins which was blatantly accessible to the questioner. They dated their family's itinerancy to the massacre of Glencoe.

Not only did Clarke fail to see the sub-classification and labels presented to him as problematic and themselves a subject for research, he also seems to have failed to test the samples from those whom either he or the Travellers had designated as "non-Romany itinerants". There is no discussion of any comparison between the results of the different samples. Ultimately the results from the so labelled "Romanies" were inconclusive as to origin. In my consultations with physical anthropologists about the results, I have been informed that it is in any case extremely difficult to suggest to what extent any of the potentially specific factors were merely the result of group endogamy – i.e. the long-term practice of Travellers choosing to marry other Travellers.

Clarke's research can be compared to that of the Italian criminologist Lombroso, who a century earlier and now laughingly discredited, measured the skull size of criminals in prison and concluded there was a criminal type. He failed to measure the skulls of "non-criminals" outside prison where similar skull sizes were also to be found.

Given that social anthropology looks at how people view themselves, a major concern should be the criteria the Travellers themselves use for membership. I have already outlined the criteria found among Travellers common to the four nationalities – descent, a commitment to certain values e.g. self-employment, geographical flexibility and usually

pollution beliefs. There is an added complexity in that Travellers or Gypsies are a minority vulnerable to the dominant
persecuting society. Already the example of the self-labelled
Scottish Travellers in Essex showed a shared discourse of key
historical moments with the gorgio questioners – e.g. the
massacre of Glencoe. The Travellers did not point to any
lesser-known historical event, but one greatly mythologised
in popular history.

I suggest that Travellers or Gypsies respond to the perceived preferences and values of gorgios or country people
when it comes to elaborating their historical origins. There is
a neat overlap between the claims of many non-Travellers
and Travellers on this question. Malinowski (1931), the anthropologist, long ago suggested that peoples may recount
and elaborate myths of origin in order to validate their current status. The peoples he studied used origin myths to
confirm hierarchy or difference.

In the case of the Travellers we find a mixture of hierarchy
and difference. Nineteenth century non-Traveller, Gorgio,
writers and commentators, themselves of the dominant English nation, used a hierarchy which placed Scottish and then
Irish Travellers lowest in their value-loaded assessment. It is a
paradox that they considered being of foreign exotic Indian
origin – translated as "real Romany" – superior to being of
local, indigenous origin. Travellers or Gypsies associated with
England or Englishness were most likely to be attributed this
foreign origin.

Travellers with a Welsh association came in the texts to be
even more worthy of the real Romany label. This privilege
may have very little to do with genetic makeup, group migrations, concentrations of populations, or distinct ways of life,
but rather with the perceptions and filters of the observer.
The real Romany has been stereotyped not only as "foreign"
but also deeply rural. Borrow, who helped to immortalise the
image of Gypsies in a mixture of fiction and non-fiction,
wrote compellingly of *Wild Wales* (1862). His descriptions of
Gypsies in urban areas in or near London did not grip the
public imagination in the same way (1874). Later, John
Sampson, an academic at Liverpool University, chose to record

the Romany dialect or language from Gypsies in North Wales. This location was geographically convenient; it being near Liverpool but sufficiently distant from an urban conurbation, in a sufficiently remote enclave in rural Wales. I suggest that the stereotyping of Gypsies and the selection of those considered authentic are affected as much by non-Gypsy texts as by empirical "reality". In turn Sampson's *The Dialect of the Gypsies of Wales* (1926) has overdetermined the identity of the "real" Gypsy.

The fact that rural Wales rather than rural Scotland or Ireland became the mythologised location of "real" exotic Gypsies could be explored in terms of the political status of the three nations in relation to England. Wales has never retained the same legal autonomy as Scotland. Is it I wonder that English writers view Welshness more benignly than the identity of the colonised Scots or the potentially autonomous Irish? Both Borrow (see Acton 1974, 65) and Sampson denigrated the Irish Travellers, especially when the latter had migrated from Ireland. Sampson referred to Irish "tinker-clans who still infest Wales" (1930, 345).

Sampson is ambivalent and patronising about Scottish Travellers. In his preface to McCormick's *The Tinkler Gypsies*, Sampson reveals his belief in a hierarchy based largely on mythical place of origin: "Yes, Gypsies are Gypsies but are Tinkler-Gypsies Romane? And if so, where abouts in the hierarchy of the Romani races should we place them?" (1907, X). While recognising that language is the main criterion used by Gypsiologists, Sampson shows an unexpected flexibility; "But Gypsies are nonetheless Gypsies because they have lost a perfect knowledge of their own tongue." (ibid). This flexibility is not shown by him elsewhere nor by others. The language used by Travellers has been taken as the major criterion by outsiders. Yet even this criterion is selectively perceived. There are ample examples of Travellers associated with Scotland or Ireland who have an extensive Romany vocabulary, Sampson noted how "the Tinker clans in Wales commonly speak both Shelta and Romani" (1930, 345). But this is seen as merely copying from or imitation of the English or Welsh Gypsies, rather than part of a heritage shared among all Travellers regardless of their national identity.

So far I have questioned whether we should attribute mainly "foreign" origins to any one national group of Gypsies within the British Isles or Ireland. I also question whether "foreignness" should be seen as the criterion for considering whether one group is any more "real" or authentic than others. There is no reason why ethnic identity should depend on foreign origins. The Travellers in Ireland have not been engaged in the same charade of authenticity as those in Britain. A foreign origin was not constructed for them by outsiders and researchers, nor did they create one for themselves. English commentators downgraded the Irish for their local origin, but it appeared acceptable to both Travellers and housedwellers within Ireland. However, there has been pressure to construct exotic indigenous origins. It is said that the Irish Traveller was descended, from the ancient Celts or a pre-Christian caste or even "displaced lords" (Barnes 1975, 231-232). Similarly in Scotland it has been said that the Travellers were the descendants of "Pictish" kings, or ancient Celts. These local mythical origins have been seen as positive in many instances.

The question arises why local origins have been seen as positive in the Irish and Scottish cases, but not in the English and Welsh cases? The answer lies in the historical circumstances of internal colonialism. I suggest that it suited Travellers in Ireland to accept and elaborate a local origin to housedwellers with whom they negotiated for work and camping land. Ireland had had enough of foreign invaders, it would be much more acceptable for housedwellers to relate to people said to be descended from landless peasants, from victims of Cromwell's brutalities or the Great Famine. The same could be said of Scottish Travellers. Scotland also had had enough of its foreign coloniser: the English. Thus in relating to housedwellers, the Scottish Travellers could successfully present themselves as descendants of victims of the massacre of Glencoe or victims of the Highland Clearances and other degradations. Scottish social scientists have tended to support such origins.

By contrast, any English Gypsies who presented themselves as victims of members of their own nation or as drop-outs from the dominant "superior race" would appear to question the values of those in power and those with whom they had a supposedly "natural" affinity. Much better if the English Gypsies could be said to be descendants of exotic outsiders who had migrated. Moreover, the Indian origin attributed to "real" Gypsies fitted neatly with the myth of the true Aryan race so vividly elaborated later in fascist Europe. The alleged link between Wales and the "true Romany" is a puzzling one. I suggest that it speaks more of the political relationship between Wales and England than of similarities or differences between the Gypsies or Travellers of each area. In addition, in the dominant English ideology, embroidered by romantic texts and stereotypes which excluded the urban industrialised and mining history of southern Wales, Welsh Gypsies were seen as real Romany partly because of their rural setting near Snowdonia.

The Irish Travellers in England have been made extremely sensitive in day-to-day encounters to the hierarchy upheld by the English, whether Gypsy or housedweller, and they have adapted accordingly. After my main fieldwork, I was taken by a housedweller supporter to meet some Travellers who were threatened with eviction from a piece of wasteland in North London. The housedweller was Irish, but I strongly suspect that the Travellers felt it necessary to respond to me as English, and a stranger. They had never met me before and knew nothing of my longterm association with Travellers. They predictably suspected me to be some official. They had migrated from Ireland, frequently travelling between the different countries, and had Irish accents. They informed me that, although many of them were "Irish", *each* family contained an English spouse called either Lee or Loveridge. I found no such evidence. Their spokesman called himself Mr Loveridge. This was unusual in several ways. For one thing, Travellers rarely if ever give their names to outsiders, especially on a first encounter. If necessary, English Travellers may present themselves as Smith – a surname which is suitably widespread and anonymous. The surnames which the

Irish Travellers presented to me have a long-established history in the British folklore literature. "Lee" is associated with "real" Welsh Romany Gypsies, while "Loveridge" is associated with "real" English Romany Gypsies. Thus Mr Loveridge, speaking in a distinct Irish accent, was in effect informing me that he was not fully foreign in so far as Irish is taken to be foreign, but that he was partially English or Welsh through the names of Loveridge and Lee. At the same time he was claiming to be exotically foreign in so far as he was claiming to be Romany of distant Indian origin. It was a brilliant manipulation of the prevailing hierarchy as seen within England. This is one micro example of how the Travellers respond to the mythical origin which most suits non-Travellers.

Within both Ireland and Scotland I have described how both Travellers and housedwellers may be comfortable with the belief in local origins. However, such origins have also been distorted, if not misused, by non-Traveller researchers, commentators and policy makers. Instead of local origins being seen as a source of respect and value, they have been used against Travellers. In Ireland, the Commission on Itinerancy (1963) helped to create the impression that Irish Travellers were merely inadequate drop-outs and therefore ripe for assimilation. Later, some Irish researchers confined Travellers to a culture of poverty. Although Patricia McCarthy (1972) has since changed her opinion (see Chapter 8), it seems that her earlier suggestions are still given greater authority in public policy.

Similarly, the work of Sharon and George Gmelch (1974, 1974, 1977) emphasised deprivation and individual drop-out theories. They did not sufficiently explore how Travellers may *choose* to continue a viable way of life. I suggest that the Travellers' deprivations were less because they were without wage-labour jobs, full-time schooling and housing, and more because they were and are deprived of geographical flexibility, legal access to camping land and the right to pursue viable self-employment and greater self-determination. The problem lies as much – if not more – with the dominant, housedwelling society, intolerant of other ways of living, of other ways of being Irish.

It may be that since independence from Britain, Ireland and the Irish are less oppressed by the English hierarchy of "real" Gypsies which places English Romany Gypsies at the top. But in so far as Irish non-Travellers, housedwellers or country people, believe that the "real" Gypsy is over the water, somewhere else and of Romany, exotic origin, they are still colluding with the British colonial classification. To say that real Travellers have to be foreign may be unwittingly asserting that "real" Travellers are English (or sometimes Welsh).

It would seem preferable for the dominant society in Ireland to show pride and respect in the Irish traditions of their own Travellers who are as real and authentic as any other Gypsies and who should be given full rights to their chosen way of life.[1]

NOTES

[1] This should also include respect for the Travellers' traditions of non-literacy. Some commentators do not recognise that a culture and community of non-literacy is very different from the position of isolated individual illiterates. There is a danger of seeing a non-literate culture as a culture of poverty or its members as a random collection of deviants, a view amply contested by S. Ní Shúinéar. Educationalists risk judging the Travellers' traditions in terms of their own ethnocentric housedwelling and schooled values. The ingenuity and ability of non-literate Travellers to adapt successfully have been grossly underestimated. The creative, inventive aspects of the Travellers' oral history and culture await further celebration rather than presumptuous denigration.

REFERENCES

Acton, T.   *Gypsy Politics and Social Change.* London: Routledge & Kegan Paul, 1974.

Adams, B., *et al.*   *Gypsies and Government Policy in England.* London: Heinemann, 1975.

Barnes, B.   "Irish Travelling People", in *Gypsies, Tinkers and Other Travellers.* R. Rehfisch (ed.). London: Academic Press, 1975, 231-56.

Borrow, G. *Wild Wales: Its People, Language and Scenery.* London: John Murray, 1862.

Borrow, G. *Romano Lavo-Lil.* London: John Murray, 1874.

Clarke, V.A. "Genetic Factors in British Gypsies", in *Genetic Variation in Britain,* vol. 12. D.F. Roberts and E. Sunderland (eds.), 1973. Symposia of the Society for the Study of Human Biology.

Clébert, J.P. *The Gypsies* (translation). Harmondsworth: Penguin, 1967.

Commission on Itinerancy *Report of the Commission on Itinerancy.* Dublin: Stationery Office, 1963.

Gmelch, G. *Change and Adaptation Among Irish Travellers.* Ph.D. dissertation, University of California, Santa Barbara, 1974.

Gmelch, G. *The Irish Tinkers: the Urbanisation of an Itinerant People.* California: Cummings, 1977.

Gmelch, S. *The Emergence and Resistance of an Ethnic Group.* Ph.D. dissertation, University of California, Santa Barbara, 1974.

Malinowski, B. "Culture", *Encyclopedia of the Social Sciences,* Vol. IV. New York: Macmillan, 1931-34, 621-46.

McCarthy, P. *Itinerancy and Poverty: A Study in the Sub-Culture of Poverty.* M.Soc.Sc. Thesis, University College, Dublin, 1972.

McCormick, A. *The Tinkler Gypsies.* Edinburgh: Dumfries, 1907.

Okely, J. "Gypsy Identity" (chapter 2), "Work and Travel" (chapter 5), in *Gypsies and Government Policy in England.* B. Adams *et al.*(eds.). London: Heinemann, 1975.

Okely, J. "Privileged, Schooled and Finished: Boarding Education for Girls", in *Defining Females.*

	S. Ardener (ed.). London: Croom Helm, 1978.
Okely, J.	*The Traveller-Gypsies.* Cambridge: Cambridge University Press, 1983.
Rehfisch, F.	*The Tinkers of Perthshire and Aberdeenshire.* Unpublished manuscript, School of Scottish Studies, Edinburgh, 1958.
Sampson, J.	*The Dialect of the Gypsies of Wales.* Oxford: Clarendon, 1926.
Sampson, J.	*The Wind on the Heath: a Gypsy Anthology.* London: Chatto and Windus, 1930.
Thompson, T.W.	"Gleanings from Constables' Accounts and other Sources", *Journal of the Gypsy Lore Society*, third series, 3(i), 1928, 34-8.
Vaux de Foletier, F. de	*Mille Ans d'Histoire des Tsiganes.* Paris: Fayard, 1970.
Vesey-Fitzgerald, B.	*Gypsies of Britain*, New Edition (first edition 1944). Newton Abbott: David and Charles, 1973.

IRISH TRAVELLERS —
A UNIQUE PHENOMENON IN EUROPE?

Donald Kenrick

Are there any groups like the Irish Travellers in continental Europe? The short answer is, yes there are. I take the following characteristics as the basic ones in seeking European comparisons with Irish Travellers: marry for preference among themselves, feel themselves to be different, have a language, dialect or variety of their own, travel in family groups (or did so until recently), are commercial or industrial rather than pastoral nomads. These characteristics are based partly on Rao (1987) and Arnold (1980).

Rao also offers a short, though not particularly simple, definition of Travellers: "endogamous nomads who are largely non-primary producers or extractors, and whose principal resources are constituted by other human populations" (Rao 1987, 1). I list at the end of the paper many of the groups that come within this definition, and describe a few of them in the paper, with a longer description of one group, the Norwegian Reisende.

TRAVELLER GROUPS

Romanies or Gypsies

The most obvious groups to compare Irish Travellers with are the Romanies or Gypsies. I refer here to groups of people who migrated from India through Persia and into Europe between the 5th and 13th centuries A.D. They are still a distinct ethnic group in most countries of Europe. But they are not one group with a similar life-style. In eastern and southern Europe they are largely sedentary and have been so for many generations. In western Europe the majority are still nomadic or are the first settled generation.

These groups include the Sinti who nomadise in Germany and neighbouring countries, the Manouche in France, Belgium and Holland, Finnish Gypsies, and various Yugoslav groups, with various traditional trades. It includes also the so-called international nomads, the Kalderash and Lovari, who in larger numbers than any others have travelled to America and Australia. There is general public awareness through books and films of the culture of Romany Gypsies, though not all the books and films give a true picture.

There are many differences within the Romany groups. At a superficial level, Spanish Romanies dance and sing in the specific flamenco style. Although you will find pictures of flamenco dancers in many caravans and homes of Gypsies outside Spain, they don't play that music and don't necessarily like listening to it. The Kalderash and Finnish Gypsy women wear long colourful dresses like the Spanish Romanies but such dresses are not found among the more than a million Romanies of eastern Europe.

Two unifying factors are found among the Romanies, whether nomadic or sedentary: the Romani language (still in daily use among the majority), and a code of cleanliness. The latter regulates, for example, the separate washing of women's and men's clothes, with both kept well away from food preparation.

The German Jenisch

Alongside the Sinti of Germany are the Jenisch of the German speaking countries, possibly the best-documented group of non-Romany nomads in Europe. The first references are about the same time as those to Romany Gypsies, circa 1400, and it is difficult to know at times which groups are being referred to. It is not possible to be sure how far back in history any group of Travellers reaches because we cannot be sure whether references in diaries or legislation to wandering persons refer to the ancestors of the wandering groups we can find today. In the first edition of his study Arnold (1980) thought that the Jenisch had begun as a group when the Romanies arrived. His theory was that until then there had been wandering craftsmen but they left their wives and children at home. When they saw the Romanies travelling with horses and carts and their whole families, they thought: what a good idea, we can take our wives and children with us when we travel. And that is how the Jenisch were formed. This would suggest rather low intelligence on the part of the Europeans and in the second revised edition of his study he is not so definite.

In fact we find that many of the commercial nomads of Europe have a winter base, a house bought, rented or more likely self-built. In times of economic hardship they may have abandoned the rented accommodation (or sold the house) and taken all their possessions with them on their journeys. It was economic necessity that later forced the English canal boatmen to sell their cottages and take their families with them on the boats, not so much to save money but as extra labour.

The Jenisch are one of the largest groups. Arnold (1980, 52) estimates there are 20,000 to 30,000 in Germany alone. It seems that the Jenisch in the past travelled outside German-speaking territories and some probably moved permanently to Scandinavia (where they became assimilated to local nomadic groups) as well as to Spain. There is also a large group of Jenisch in France (called Barengre by the Romanies) who have kept a separate identity. There are subgroups among the Jenisch, including the basket and sievemakers of Lower Alsace and Pfalz who merit further study.

The Swiss Manouche and Jenisch have aroused a lot of interest recently for two reasons. First, it was discovered that large numbers had been kidnapped – I think this is the right word – by the Church and given to Swiss families. The parents were told their children had died and the children were told that their parents had died. When they grew up some of these children made efforts to find out about their origins and made contact with Gypsy families. They represented an educated group who got together, set up an organisation, produced a magazine and campaigned for the reuniting of families and a stop to the fostering programme. Second, the Swiss Jenisch took part in the Second World Romany Congress (held in Geneva) and – together with the Irish Travellers – are one of the few non-Romany groups to identify with the Romanies and to have regular contact with international Romany organisations.

The Mercheros or Quincailleros of Spain

I will call them "Mercheros" which is their preferred name, rather than "Quincailleros" which has a pejorative meaning. The Mercheros are not the only socially distinct group existing in Spain. León-Ignacio (1974) names 6 others: Agotos, Jordanos, Monantes, Pasiesos, Vaqueiros de Alzeda, Maragatos Morenos.

There is no definite information about their origin. There is a tendency in Spain, as elsewhere, to assume that these nomadic groups came into existence at the time of the first laws directed against wandering ex-soldiers and displaced peasants which we find in most countries. But this does not mean that commercial nomads did not exist before that time.

We have a certain amount of information about them from León-Ignacio's study. The majority travelled regular routes calling at the same villages where they seem to have been made welcome. The women bought animal skins which they later sold to hat factories. Because they came so regularly the peasants would keep the skins of (say) rabbits they shot until the Mercheros arrived to buy them, or more likely barter them for the services the men did, generally repair work. This is one example that shows that the nomads and their sedentary clients were mutually useful. With the migration of their customers to the towns around 1950 they were forced to follow them. Until then Merchero families tended to travel on their own – a nuclear family including only unmarried children – and keep very much to themselves. This probably helped their economy, there was less competition for customers, and made it easier to find lodging.

The migration into towns has led to the emergence of Merchero quarters or at least quarters with a substantial Merchero population. One such was La Perona near Barcelona, a shanty town with Spanish Gypsies, Kalderash Gypsies, Mercheros and a few migrant Andalucians. It has to be accepted that once in town some young Mercheros were unable to adapt and turned to petty crime to survive.

The Spanish Larousse gives as its definition of Quinqui (Quincaillero): "delincuente contra la propriedad que opera en peguenas bandas" (criminal against property who operates in small bands) (León-Ignacio 1974, 24). One Merchero, El Lute, became a sort of Robin Hood figure in the 1970's. In prison, he renounced crime and there was a national, indeed international, campaign to secure his pardon and release.

There are two separate groups of Merchero with different physical characteristics. One is blond with blue eyes (possibly originally German Jenisch) and the other has dark hair. They do not intermarry and did not mix when they travelled. León-Ignacio recounts one local experience of a day nursery catering for settled Merchero children in a suburb where the two groups of children fought each other daily for several weeks until they became friends.

In a way that resembles perhaps the Burakumin in Japan, the dark Merchero are distinguished from Spaniards because they are known to be Merchero and not through any physical characteristics or dress. An informant said: I am a Merchero because I belong to the family X. I have seen nothing in print about their language, which is said to be Spanish with some words of their own.

The Norwegian 'Reisende'

Thanks to the work of 19th century writers, and in this century Ragnhild Schlüter, we are quite well informed about the Travellers of Norway. There are two groups of Travellers in Norway, both well established, and distinct from the recent immigrations of Romanies: the long-distance Travellers and the short-distance Travellers.

The long-distance Travellers (Taterne) speak Norwegian with many words borrowed from Romani. They are generally considered to be the descendants of the first Romanies who came to Norway in the 15th and 16th centuries, and intermarried over the years with both settled and nomadic Norwegians. (We can assume that this is not the only case where Romanies, threatened with expulsion or even execution for being a Romany, have merged with local nomads for safety). The short-distance Travellers (Fantene) speak Norwegian with an exotic vocabulary from various sources (Iversen 1945). I will say a little more about the language later. There are records of nomadic immigrants coming from Sweden and Germany and these have been absorbed, probably into both groups. In this century the distinction between the two groups is less important and Schlüter considers that the second group has largely assimilated with the general population (personal communication).

The Norwegian Travellers certainly existed in 1276 when a law forbade people to give them lodging, and ferrymen to carry them. This was 200 years before the first Romanies came to Scandinavia. They engaged in what were considered unclean professions; chimney sweeps, horse castrators, hangmen and skinners. Some of the men developed from horse castrators to doing general veterinary work and making horseshoes, and some were attached to army regiments in this role. They made products from hair, did weaving, decorated knives, repaired clocks (the only time I have come across this as a nomadic trade), metal work, including gutters and later, ventilation. The women made and sold baskets and herbal medicines. They peddled both the craftwork of the men and things bought wholesale in the towns and they sold retail, including table cloths and writing paper. Schlüter reckons, based on some individual case histories, that these specialist workers were joined by deserters, unmarried mothers, escaped apprentices, bankrupt farmers, and dismissed farm labourers, to form the Travelling community. The same has been said about the Spanish Mercheros.

The following ethnographic notes (Schlüter 1990) do not claim to be scientific but give a picture of the life of the

Reisende which may bring them to life. Some had handcarts and all the family walked alongside, others had two-wheeled carts drawn by horses until they were forbidden to have horses. Later bicycles came into use and after 1950 caravans and cars. In winter sledges were used, pulled by horses. Others had boats and sailed down the coast in the summer, trading from village to village as pedlars and craftsmen. Some families travelled on the regular coastal routes. In winter they stayed on land.

A characteristic feature was that all families took their own bedding, as they were afraid of the bedding in the lodging houses. From 1920 tents came into use. They travelled in extended family units of 20-30 people. Brides joined their husbands' families. One reason for travelling in a larger group was protection against attack. The Reisende kept in contact with other families by the use of "patrijals" (a Romani word) to show where they had gone. These were signs made with a combination of sticks and stones. In winter signs were traced in the snow. I hear that many have now graduated to CB radio and car phones as a means of communication.

The horse was very important. It was the prime means of transport but could be sold to buy a boat, or in winter to buy a hut. Norwegian government policy for decades has been to stop the Travellers keeping horses and thereby curtail their travelling and change their way of life. Many of the Norwegian Travellers were – and are – reasonably well-off. This is borne out by the various accoutrements of the horse which are both ornamental and expensive, whether in leather or metal. Another item – expensive when first bought – was a decorative "coffee case" to hold the essentials for making and drinking coffee. These were inherited.

The women's dresses were traditionally colourful with several layers of skirts, though not as varied as in the dress of the Finnish Romanies today. Brooches, necklaces and earrings were popular so that wealth could be carried rather than deposited in a bank, though the large gold engagement rings would not normally be sold. The men wore a coloured scarf, leather waistcoat with silver buttons and a thick gold ring.

This men's gold ring, unlike the women's ring, had the special role of being pawned when money was short.

These are the only non-Romany industrial nomadic group, apart from the Irish Travellers, credited with a musical tradition. Songs were sung at night around a fire. A popular theme was the beauty of Traveller girls. One song composed around 1890 is known by all Travellers. The fiddle (violin) is still a popular instrument. Many Traveller violinists became famous in the 19th century and are still remembered today in the names of dance tunes.

They were apparently popular with some villagers, but were evidently not liked by the authorities. I have mentioned a thirteenth century law. There is a period when it is not possible to distinguish between laws against Romanies and those directed against the indigenous nomads, but as the comparatively few Romanies were either driven out or left Norway by 1700 (or disappeared into the local nomadic community) we can assume that, for example, the Pedlars' Hunt (Fantejakt) of 1710 was directed against the indigenous nomadic families. This was a hunt organised by the authorities over 3 counties to seek out Travellers and lock them up. Individual Travellers and their families were locked up in workhouses after these were established from 1733 onwards. Apart from having to work, they were taught to read and write so that they could be confirmed. These "Traveller Hunts" were common in Scandinavia and perhaps were modelled on the Hunts for Gypsies held in Germany and Holland. The last recorded hunt in Norway was as late as 1907.

In the 19th century a priest called Sundt became the government expert on Travellers after a five week tour on a research grant, during which he met only five and these hardly spoke to him. He later met many more and wrote about them extensively (Sundt 1852). I find his descriptions of their religion, e.g. that they worshipped the moon and a god called Alako, very doubtful and would like to find confirmation of this in another unrelated source. Sundt was one of the few who wrote about the Travellers and his descriptions have been used by writers ever since, by Ibsen, Strindberg and Hans Christian Andersen amongst others. These fictional

Travellers have shaped the opinions of many Scandinavians who have never seen the real persons at close hand.

Norwegian government policy was to break up the community. In 1855 alone the Fantefond took 256 children away from their parents and placed them with fosterparents. Some settled Travellers hide their identity because of discrimination while others have "come out" such as the painter Karl Wang and a rock musician Age Aleksandere.

The Dutch Woonwagenbewoners

Holland has a large population of caravan dwellers, who do not identify themselves as Romanies (T. Acton, personal communication). I don't propose to say anything about them other than that the only one I interviewed had travelled to Copenhagen and stopped on the caravan site built for Danish nomads, suggesting links with the Traveller communities outside Holland. For many years however the Dutch Travellers have lived in caravans too large for the sites which local authorities have built for them. Because of a belief that they are the offspring of Dutch housedwellers who took to the road in the 19th century there has been little interest in studying their customs, though there is a considerable literature on their housing problems.

TRAVELLER CULTURE

I now look at topics across the groups. There is no common deep culture shared by all the nomads of Europe or even by all the non-Romany groups. The extreme attention to cleanliness of food and clothing common to all is more likely due to the necessity for this when travelling, than to a common origin and common set of beliefs.

Death

Arnold (1980) notes that Jenisch to whom he talked do not see the soul of a dead person (mulo) as a continuation of the deceased but as a separate entity, and one to be avoided.

They get away from funerals as fast as possible. They do, however, attend funerals in large numbers. It has been noted, perhaps not surprisingly, that recently settled Jenisch attend funerals in lower numbers than nomadic families, as they are not such important occasions for meeting relatives and friends.

There is a contrast here in the avoidance of the dead with the Spanish Mercheros who used to camp quite happily near cemeteries, as do the Gypsies in Leeds. León-Ignacio (1974) cites one who used to carry bodies across Spain, presumably of Spanish people who had died away from their home town or village. One recorded custom, certainly not unique to the Mercheros, is to place an object belonging to the dead person in their coffin. A recent report of a Romany funeral from Norway refers to the placing in the coffin of the deceased's hat and walking stick as well as a toilet bag with toothpaste and deodorant (Schlüter, personal communication).

Marriage

Marriages amongst the Mercheros are initiated by the uncle of the young men. At the marriage party men and women eat separately. The bride takes food and drink from the men's tables and carries it off to share with the women. In the case of the Yugoslav Cherhari – who were recently in London – the initial steps in marriage are taken by male friends or relatives of the prospective bridegroom. Many will see the parallel with Balkan, and I expect older Irish, tradition. I remember in the autobiography of "Peig" (Peig Sayers) that she didn't find out until much later which of the three men who came to supper one evening was her intended husband.

But marriage customs vary enormously even in the same area. The Kalderash have a form of "bride price" where the father of the groom pays a large sum of money to the father of the bride, more than enough to cover the wedding ceremony which is paid for by the bride's father, while among the Bulgarian Romanies the bride brings a large dowry with her.

English Romanies traditionally had a form of elopement while the parents pretended they did not know what was going on. In Finland even today a couple will elope, and have to stay away from their parents for months – often years – before there is grudging acceptance of the marriage.

Language

The Norwegian Travellers have two separate languages, both varieties of Norwegian. The first called "Romani" has a vocabulary of some 1,250 words of which the majority are Romani and the rest loans from the other variety, Rodi. Examples of Romani words are *bakro* (sheep), *faro* (town), *paena* (sister). The second language, Rodi, has some 1,400 words excluding those formed merely by disguising Norwegian words. New compounds can be formed for new concepts e.g. for a photograph – *skitterskalo* (lit. sight-glass). For the same concept (photograph) there is also *biali-glarom*. These examples show the ability of the language to coin words for new ideas.

This is similar to the practice of English Romanies, who have, for example, a word for elephant – *bori bilavangustra* – though one can hardly imagine a time when they might want to discuss elephants without the Gorgios understanding. The Kalderash and most Yugoslav and Bulgarian Gypsies are quite happy to use the borrowed words *fotograf* and *elefanto*. (The original Indian word seems to have been forgotten). There are also many words formed simply by adding a syllable to a Norwegian word.

I have avoided looking at sedentary Romany populations as I have taken "travelling" to be one of the main characteristics of the Irish Travellers. In their way of life Irish Travellers are closer to nomadic Romany groups than the latter are to sedentary Romany groups. Of course, a great deal depends upon the criteria used. As far as language and physical characteristics the nomadic and settled Romanies are close; as far as way of life is concerned, nomadism seems to affect groups in a similar way regardless of their ethnic origin.

Origins

I have not come across many legends of non-Romany Travellers concerning their origin, although most nomadic groups of Africa or Asia have such explanations, not necessarily true, of how they arose (Rao, passim). There are a great many legends about the origin of the Romanies in the literature, collected both from themselves and Gorgios.

There are at least three ways in which indigenous nomadic groups could theoretically have been formed:

(i)   in Asia at least, as survivors of hunter-gatherers who stayed as hunter-gatherers up to the present time while the rest of the population became sedentary or pastoral nomads;

(ii) as an indigenous minority suppressed by invaders and surviving by commercial nomadism, or a specialist sedentary occupational group which became nomadic as a result of economic competition (if this group then moves into another country it will also become ethnically distinct);

(iii) as a migrant minority surviving by continuing commercial nomadism wherever they may be.

The Romanies of western Europe fall into this last class. We can compare them with the East African Indians who came to England and after a short time survived economically in similar ways to how they had lived in Africa, running small shops and post offices and gradually taking over newsagents and chemists from the Welsh of an earlier migration.

I think commercial nomads can only survive as long as they fill an economic or social need of the larger sedentary society. As Rao says, when society changes commercial nomads have to change with it and find new gaps they can fill (Rao 1987, 23). Instead of shoeing horses they can buy second-hand cars in one part of the country where they are cheap and sell them in another part where they are dear.

THE MAJORITY SOCIETY AND TRAVELLERS

Members of the majority society hold particular images of Travellers. For example, Norwegian Reisende women are thought to be sensual, seductive and have powers over men; the men are thought to be thieves, fight with knives; all are thought to have a wanderlust, an urge for freedom and to live close to nature. In Norway the indigenous nomads are usually called *omstreifere* (wanderers) by official sources. Schlüter (1990) quotes many newspapers with articles about crimes allegedly committed by these *omstreifere* or warning against them.

Works dealing with the history of the Romany Gypsies mention early warning systems in the Middle Ages against nomads, such as the ringing of church bells (Journal of the Gypsy Lore Society 3, xii, 134). This was probably at a time when as a result of war local villagers had no money to trade with the nomads and saw themselves as possibly having to share their meagre supply of food with them.

I was reminded of this in Bulgaria recently (though before the political changes). In Bulgaria the majority of Romanies have been settled for generations and are an ethnic minority with members at all levels of society. Some did manage to continue a semi-nomadic life and the fear of nomads persisted at least among the authorities. In a railway station by the ticket office was a large notice: ANYONE SEEING NOMADIC GYPSIES [skitni tsigani] SHOULD REPORT THEIR PRESENCE IMMEDIATELY TO THE POLICE (phone number given).

Apart from the Spanish example referred to above, dictionary definitions of the various groups are not particularly pejorative. German dictionaries see the Jenisch as nomads who speak a Gaunersprache, a feature nearly always mentioned.

Salmonsen's Danish encyclopaedia of 1938 (Marke and Raunkjaer (1939)) says of the Natmandsfolk (not in itself a very complimentary term): "A nomadic people living from (previously) despised jobs, supplemented by begging and thieving" ("Et Vandringsfolk levende af . . . foragtede Arbejder suppleret med Tiggeri og Tyveri") and of the Norwegian Travellers (under the term Fanter): "People still suffered from the plague of this nuisance at the end of the 19th century" ("Endnu i Slutn. af det. 19 Aarh. fû-ûlte man Plagen ved dette Uvaesen"). The Norwegian priest Sundt subtitled his work on the Norwegian Travellers in 1852: "Contribution to knowledge about the lowest levels of society" ("de laveste Samfundsforholdet") (Sundt 1852).

CONCLUSION

To summarise, there are groups in Europe with a similar lifestyle to the Irish Travellers. Some of these are definitely Romany, some may be and some are definitely not. To say that they are not Romany does not mean that no Romany has ever intermarried into them. Studying them does suggest to me that there were commercial nomads in Europe independently of the Romany immigration and that they have survived till today as separate ethnic groups. All are having to adapt to a changing unfriendly majority society and few are getting much support in this adaptation.

APPENDIX: TRAVELLING GROUPS IN EUROPE

1.   Indigenous nomadic groups:

Jenisch (Germany, Switzerland, France)
Woonwagenbewoners (Holland)
Reisende (Fantene) (Norway)
Reisende (Denmark)
Quinquis (Spain)
Camminanti (Italy)
Travellers (Ireland)
Karrner (Austria)

2.   Groups which are probably the result of intermarriage between Romanies and indigenous nomadic groups:

Travellers (Scotland)
Tattare (Reisende) (Sweden)
Reisende (Taterne) (Norway)

3.   Groups which are probably Romanies who no longer speak Romani:

Shatravaci (Yugoslavia)
Rudari (Rumania and elsewhere)
Bayash (Hungary and elsewhere)

4.   Groups which are definitely Romanies but who no longer speak Romani (i.e. even the oldest members of the group do not speak Romani):

Gitanos (Spain, Portugal, Southern France)
Romanies (Romany chals) (U.K.)
Bosha (Armenia)
Grebenari (Bulgaria)

N.B. I exclude the "svetski" of Czechoslovakia as my contacts with them suggest that they were what in U.K. we would call "Showmen" i.e. circus and fairground operators.

REFERENCES

Arnold, H.   *Fahrendes Volk.* Landau/Pfalz: Pfälzische
                                    Verlag, 1980.

Arnold, H.   *Randgruppen des Zigeunervolkes.* (Preprint of
                                    Arnold 1980), 1975.

Bonilla, K.   "The Quinquis", *Journal of the Gypsy Lore
                                    Society* (4th Series), vol. 1. pt.2. 1976, 86-93.

Iversen, R.   *Secret Languages in Norway,* pts 1 and 2. Oslo:
                                    Norske Videnskapsakademi, 1944, 1945.

Kenrick, D.   "Eilert Sundt and the Norwegian Travel-
                                    lers", *Roma,* vol.3, no.2 Chandigarh, 1977.

León-Ignacio   *Los Quinquis.* Barcelona: Ediciones 29, 1974.

Marke, A. and Raunkjaer, P.   *Den Lille Salmonsen,* Vol. 8. Copenhagen:
                                    Schultz, 1939.

Mertens, J.   *En Belgique au 15-ème siècle, des Marchands
                                    Ambulants: les Teutens.* Études Tsiganes (pt
                                    3). Paris, 1990.

Midböe, O.   *Eilert Sundt og Fantesaken.* Oslo: Universitets
                                    Forlaget, 1968.

Rao, A. (ed.)   *The Other Nomads.* Cologne: Böhlau, 1987.

Rehfisch, F. (ed.)   *Gypsies, Tinkers and other Travellers.* U.K.:
                                    Academic Press, 1975.

Schlüter, R.   *De Reisende - En Glemt Minoritet.* Levanger:
                                    Laererhögskole, 1990.

Sundt, E.   *Fante-eller Landstrygerfolket i Norge.* Oslo:
(ed. Christophersen)   Gyldendal (Reprint of 1852 edition), 1974.

CATEGORISING IRISH TRAVELLERS

Thomas Acton

INTRODUCTION — UNWRITING HISTORY

Deference to a people's own account of its identity, origin and history is generally wise, especially when that account is also generally accepted in the academic and policy-making worlds. One should only be driven to challenge a people's account when one wishes to question the fundamental terms of reference within which it is built up: when one is not so much contradicting as deconstructing it. If the following paper is read as saying "So Acton asserts that, after all, Irish Travellers are Gypsies", then it will have failed in its purpose. It would be more to the point to say that this paper asserts that, in the sense in which it is said that Irish Travellers are not Gypsies, not even Gypsies are Gypsies.

What is proposed here is not a specific hypothesis about Irish Travellers but an alternative understanding of the history of Gypsies/Travellers between the two major genocidal episodes of the 16th and 20th centuries. Its consequences for our understanding of Irish Traveller history are secondary to a hoped-for contribution to the general understanding of European racism and aggression over the past four centuries, by unmasking the way in which the need to conceal genocidal acts from European self-perception has hidden from consciousness the slaughter and oppression which are the condition of both the birth and the continuance of the nation-state. So large an hypothesis can scarcely be successfully defended empirically in so brief a paper, nor can it yet be expected to command widespread support. But in so far as the position presented here is a logical alternative among the array on offer concerning the contribution of ethnicity to Traveller identity, this paper may clarify matters even for those who reject it, by enabling us to present a typology of the positions taken up in academic writing.

NON-GYPSY TRAVELLERS?

The Irish Travellers are only one of a number of groups across Europe, mostly involved in commercial nomadism, for whom the starting point of the contemporary social definition of their identity is the assertion both by themselves and by others that they are not Gypsies. Such groups include the Bargoens-speaking Dutch Woonwagenbewoner, the Jenisch and the Scandinavian Tattare or Resende speaking varieties of Rotwelsch or Rodi, and perhaps the Quinqui in Spain. The Beash or Boyash may be an anomalous case in that inside Romania they traditionally denied Romani identity, but more recently Beash groups who have migrated outside of Romania have accepted the label of Gypsies (Papp 1982, Acton 1989). These groups all have ethnic languages of their own, marked to a greater or lesser extent by Romani influence (except in the extreme case, Beash, an archaic Romanian dialect from the Banat region where the need to avoid slave status probably led to a conscious excising of all Romani influence). Alongside them there are also groups with similar dialects, "Para-Romani" in the sense of Cortiade (1991), of whom some members assert they are Gypsies and others not, such as the Scottish Travellers, or who assert (at least some of the time) that they are Gypsies, but whose Romani authenticity is denied by other Gypsy groups.

There has been a racist argument that all of these groups must be partly of Gypsy origin because only that can explain their nomadism. This was the theory of the compromised German social scientist Arnold (1961, 1975) who argued that something like a Gypsy gene both explained their nomadism, and, through intermarriage, the coming of other nomadic groups in Europe. This view presents clear continuities with the racial science of the National Socialist era in Germany and – at least for a few years yet – needs no rebuttal in a scholarly paper. Since the economic anthropology of commercial nomadism is now a well-developed field of study (Acton 1985, Rao 1987) we no longer need genetic explanations of Gypsy nomadism, still less of that of "other" Travellers. The problematic of Arnold's *Randgruppen des Zigeunervolkes* (1975) has been dissolved, or so it might seem. We no longer need, as Okely (1983) points out, the hypothesis of an "exotic" origin, to explain the current realities of Traveller life, or even to assert (in a sociological sense, rather than according to the Mandla criteria of English Race Discrimination case law) that Traveller groups have their own ethnic identity. Unfortunately, Okely has been widely, if unfairly, misread (not least by lawyers) to be saying simply that "Travellers" are not part of a/the Gypsy "race" (Acton 1990).

The trouble is that the phenomena for which Arnold presented a geneticist explanation remain in being even if currently unproblematised. It is still the case that there are a number of Traveller groups across Europe who start their account of who they are, by saying who they are not, viz. Gypsies. To whom are they trying to prove what, and why? Moreover the dialects of most of those groups (the Beash excluded) do show some Romani influence, while their organisation of washing and cleanliness usually show similar systems of differentiation of bowls and other prohibitions to those of Romani-identifying groups world-wide. Both the latter points, though sometimes denied, are true of the Irish Travellers.

Traditionally, however, the scholarly approach to Irish Travellers did not so much repudiate the racism which asserts that "race" can explain culture, as simply deny that Irish Travellers were of Gypsy "race" – as though the latter would have explained something, had it been true. Essentially, what we find is a simple inversion of the Arnold position, rather than any refutation of it. The links between Irish Travellers and Romani-identifying groups are often simply assumed away. For example, Macalister (1937, 131), in what still astonishingly stands as the standard work on Gammon, tells us that he has omitted from his Irish Traveller "Shelta" vocabulary a considerable number of lexical items with a Romani origin which were present in word-lists collected from Travellers. He feels entitled to assume that these words are recent borrowings because "Tinkers" are not "gypsies" – and thus to correct the evidence to support this conclusion.

More recently, Williams (1986) excluded Minceir in South Wales *even as a comparison group* in a study of the genetics of Gypsies in South Wales on the grounds that her target population (primarily from South Welsh Romanichal Prices and their kin) ". . . were all familiar with their ancestral way of life, and quickly distinguished themselves as separate from the Irish tinkers [sic] whom they considered to be dirty and dishonest. On Leckwith Heath in Cardiff, where the Romany gypsies [sic] and Irish tinkers lived apparently side by side, there was a clearly-defined demarcation line over which neither party crossed." Williams seems to assume that such a crude Romani/tinker distinction can be generalised on a worldwide basis, and makes comparisons of her sample with "true gypsies of Romany origin" to assert that there is "substantial evidence in favour of the genetic affinity of gypsy populations with those of India" despite very considerable heterogeneity among the genetic data-sets quoted – a heterogeneity within which in fact genetic data from Irish Traveller groups elsewhere (Crawford 1975) could be not uncomfortably located. (Crawford himself fails to draw this conclusion because, unlike Williams, he uses a very limited range of Romani comparison data.) In short, if Williams was looking for measures of genetic difference between her sample and surrounding populations, the Irish Travellers next door should have been the first group with which to compare them; that she does not is a measure of the fact that the assertion that "Irish Travellers are not Gypsies" is as much part of a racist scheme of categories as Arnold's assertion that all European Traveller groups must have been produced by inter-marriage with Gypsies.

The assertion that "Irish Travellers are not Gypsies" is also not without a political agenda. If the attribution of minority rights is predicated on a distinct ethnic identity, and the possession of a distinct ethnic identity is only allowed upon proof of "exotic" "racial" origins, then it can be argued that because Irish Travellers "are not Gypsies", they are therefore "not an ethnic group" and therefore discrimination against them is not racist, and general arguments about the oppression of Gypsies by Europeans have no relevance.

Similar arguments are made about Woonwagenbewoner in the Netherlands and various groups of Resende in Scandinavia. In the past, some Travellers from such groups have argued, as have many Irish Travellers, that they are local people and should not be treated as an ethnic group of any kind; though one can also find in the past the persecution of Gypsies contrasted rather than identified with racism (as in South Africa) by English Gypsies and their friends (Dodds 1966, 137, 142, 162). As the "race relations" political strategy has been legitimised, so such groups have progressively retreated from this position into claiming an ethnic identity (once it is likely that such a claim will mitigate rather than increase discrimination) and even to explore previously denied "exotic" elements in their language or culture. Perhaps we may see the position of the Beash in Hungary and other countries outside Romania, where it has become in some sense "obvious" that "they are Gypsies after all" as a culmination of this process of reidentification (Acton 1989).

This "rediscovery" of cultural group identity, though it may be required to prove that one constitutes a group for the purposes of anti-discrimination legislation, may still lay one open to actual discrimination as well. To see the dangers we need look no further than recent publications from the U.K. Department of the Environment, which produce, as the latest conceptual reincarnation of the "True Gypsy", the idea of the "Traditional Traveller". A research consultancy report published by the Department of the Environment (Clark and Todd 1991 a and b) effectively recommends ethnic segregation on Gypsy Caravan Sites, with the right to provision for those who are not "Traditional Travellers" removed or separated (Acton 1991). Subsequently after a pilot of a reformed method of carrying out the "Biannual Survey" of Gypsies in England, the OPCS (Office of Population Cenuses and

Surveys) has advised that local authority counting staff include the following "Types of Traveller": "Romany Gypsies, Irish Travellers, Long-Distance Travellers, Gypsies in transit through the district, Settled Gypsies, Non-local Gypsies, Gypsies on fairground sites, Gypsies on ordinary (non-Gypsy) caravan/mobile home sites, New Age Travellers" (Green 1991, 67). Furthermore, parallelling Clark and Todd, the OPCS suggest that in future "New Age Travellers" be counted separately from the "Gypsy Count", the step needed to prepare for their exclusion from entitlement to sites. The principle of the 1968 Caravan Sites Act, of a right for Travellers to travel regardless of their ethnic origin, is now under serious threat.

CURRENT ACADEMIC ACCOUNTS OF GYPSY/TRAVELLER ETHNIC IDENTITY – A TENTATIVE TYPOLOGY

This threat is seen as dangerous by supporters of Travellers such as those in this volume, whether, like Okely, they minimise the importance of ethnic origin, or like Kenrick they see cultural identity as vital to community defence. In order to clarify these various positions, and to distinguish that of this paper, I now present a tentative typology of possible positions on the relationship of "origins" to current group or ethnic identity among Travellers, as exemplified in particular texts (see Table 1).

On the far-right hand (Col. 5) is the position that might strictly be termed "racist". The policy-makers in the next column (Col. 4) would probably wish to claim they are as anti-racist as anyone, but they still wish to continue with ethnically specific, or discriminatory policies. The most far-reaching opposition to such policies comes from the Okely "de-ethnicising" position (Col. 1), which can simply deny any foundation at all in reality or knowledge for the categories of this discrimination. Okely criticises the Kenrick/Bakewell/Hancock position (Col. 3) as an "exoticising" of Gypsies which opens the door for discriminatory politics and racism.

TABLE 1

	Column 1	Column 2	Column 3	Column 4	Column 5
	Okely 1983 Mayall 1990	Acton 1985, 1990, Ní Shúinéar 1990	Kenrick & Bakewell 1990 Hancock 1984, 1991	Clark & Todd 1991a, 1991b, Green 1991 E.M. Williams 1986	Odley 1984 Vesey-Fitzgerald 1973, Arnold 1961, 1975
Believe "exotic" ethnic origins have important causal effects and explanatory functions	No	Yes	Yes	Yes	Yes
Believe "exotic" ethnic origins clearly demarcate distinct current ethnic groups	No	No	Yes	Yes	Yes
Support social discrimination on the basis of "exotic" ethnic origin	No	No	No	Yes	Yes
Believe in genetic determination of "exotic" social and psychological characteristics	No	No	No	No	Yes

This typology has been developed in correspondence with colleagues, and an earlier version was presented at the Gypsy Lore Society conference in July 1991; I must acknowledge many helpful comments. I should emphasize that it is a typology of texts, rather than writers, since writers are not always consistent, and anyway positions may be being modified during present controversies, my own not least. And I apologise in advance to writers who think I have fitted them in wrongly.

The answer that can be given from the Kenrick viewpoint is that by failing to establish the ethnic specificity of ethnic groups, the Okely position also by default opens the path to discrimination, by cutting away the grounds for the legal and political defence of Gypsies against racism, by denial of difference and the historical roots and development of culture.

TRAVELLER GROUPS AS
THE PRODUCT OF HISTORY

The resolution presented to this controversy by this paper is to disentangle and disaggregate the various historical positions which are tied together in these two positions to assert that a more realist account of the history of Travellers in Europe can be given, which asserts the specific causative importance of real historical ethnic origins, without asserting that they are finally determinant of present ethnic identity (or are in any way a valid basis for social discrimination).

The key period of history to understand the development of Traveller group identities is the genocidal purge of the 16th century, *o pervo poraimos*. Gypsy history is often presented as though it were one continuous stream of murderous marginalisation and exclusion; but this is misleading. In fact it is marked by two relatively short periods of intense genocidal persecution – let us say 1520-1600 (varying a little between countries) and 1930-1945. These are distinct in character from the more routinised discrimination and harassment at other times, even though these periods are also marked by occasional crises and atrocities, and, until the mid-18th century, the occasional renewal of genocidal laws. The fact that genocidal laws have to be renewed fifty or a hundred years after being first passed, is surely a sign that the genocide has not been successfully carried out recently.

In the century after Gypsies first appeared in Western Europe there are certainly individual Gypsy-Gajo conflicts and prejudice – but they are contained within the general framework of social order. Gypsies clearly possessed a sophisticated political leadership which was able to treat with kings, popes, and emperors to obtain or forge the charters, licences and juridical recognition (MacRitchie 1894, chs 4-5, Vesey-Fitzgerald 1973, ch. 2) which so amused 19th century Gypsylorists, but which were hardly a joke at the time; they also entertained and practised medicine at royal courts. They may well have known, as the monks of Forli suggested in 1422, that their country of origin was in fact India, and the fact that we have at least two very early Romani vocabularies shows that at that stage they did not keep their language a secret (Vaux de Foletier 1970, 18, 25).

By 1600 all of this sophisticated leadership, all of this contribution to scientific, medical and cultural life had been dispersed as though it had never been. Within a generation everything changed. First of all there were laws expelling Gypsies from various countries in Western Europe – but these could not work when other countries were also expelling Gypsies, and from the mid-16th century we find laws in various states making it a capital offence merely to be a Gypsy (Liégeois 1987, pp 90-94). Although the majority of Gypsies who were judicially murdered under such laws probably died in the 16th century, the laws themselves were often not formally repealed till the 19th century, and we find isolated examples of Gypsies suffering under them (as well as being subject to much harsher treatment than Gajes under other laws) up to the 18th century.

It is difficult now to comprehend how great a catastrophe this must have been for Romani people in Western Europe. It must have been for them as though they were Jews and Hitler had won the last war, and subsequently Jews could only continue to live as long as they were not known as Jews to state authorities. Gypsy groups in Western Europe today are the survivors of a genocide that has never been repudiated by the states involved; a genocide which fixed popular images of Gypsies as thieves, necromancers, pagans and child-stealers as the common state of knowledge. For a couple of hundred years there was virtually no inter-country Gypsy migration in Europe, apart from small movements of refugees or indentured labour to the Americas. And even the ethnic character of the "pretended Egyptians'" specificity was simply denied. After the 16th century we find no further vocabularies of Romani published till the 18th century when Europeans (re)-"discover" Romani and its Indian roots. Prior to that we find assertions that the Gypsies have no language of their own, but only a made-up gibberish, mere jargon or slang (Hancock 1988); and "Gypsy vocabularies" of the 17th and early 18th centuries, such as those associated with popular accounts of the life of Bampfylde Moore Carew (Black 1913, 31- 3), actually give us vocabularies of thieves' slang almost as devoid of Indian-derived elements as Beash. Relative darkness of skin-pigmentation was asserted to be the result of rubbing on ointments.

One consequence of this unrepented genocidal episode is that when in the 19th and 20th centuries scholars (including some themselves of Romani ethnicity) began to realise from the study of old records something of the scale of what had happened to Gypsies in the 16th century, they have tended to explain it in terms of supposed characteristics of the Gypsy community derived from the post-genocidal image of Gypsies which they have projected back onto the pre-genocidal community. Thus we are informed that non-Gypsies resented Gypsies' non-adherence to the established church, or their tendency to thievery. A moment's thought, however, should lead us to ask the unanswerable question as to why, if it were these supposed characteristics of the Gypsy community that led to their persecution, they did not do so in the same degree in the first century of their presence in Western Europe. Equally, I do not wish to suggest that these persecutions, though undoubtedly racist, can be explained psychologically simply by referring to European racism, as though that suddenly burgeoned all of its own in the mid-16th century.

It was not Gypsies or Europeans who had changed, but Europe itself. It is essential that we do not see the first Gypsy holocaust as some private Gypsy tragedy caused by the character of the Gypsy community, but as part of the general economic and political history of the era which saw the beginning of agricultural capitalism and the foundation of the nation-state, which were accompanied by inflation at hitherto unknown rates, and the start of unemployment in the modern sense (as opposed to the underemployment in times of scarcity in feudal society). These phenomena led to religious and ethnic hatreds and scapegoating of which Gypsies were very far from the only victims.

In England, between the Black Death in 1348 and the beginning of the 16th century, the real wages of agricultural workers tripled. Between 1485 and 1601, however, while prices rose 6 times (an inflation fuelled by the looting of gold from the Americas), agricultural wages only doubled in money terms; that is to say in real terms they went right back to what they had been 250 years before, at a time when society as a whole was getting much richer (Tawney 1912, 1924). Landowners, instead of seeing themselves as leaders of a community which had to be fed from its land, began to see themselves as owners of a capital asset; and the way to maximise profit on that was to minimise labour costs – and the most obvious route to that was to switch from arable to sheep farming. There was a massive shake-out of agricultural labour, providing the human resources for a growth of the mercantile economy. In fact, during the Tudor period there was a transfer of income and wealth from the poor to the rich on a scale that makes Mrs Thatcher look like a socialist.

This economic shake-up had profound social consequences. Social control required considerable extra resources; the state had to be protected by a professional standing army and navy, and the development of the Elizabethan secret police. The labour that was shaken out from agriculture did not go swiftly into new employment; nor, after Henry VIII, were the monasteries there to absorb or succour the indigent. All these redundant labourers could do was to migrate to whatever economic opportunities were available, and in betweenwhiles beg. The "sturdy beggars" and the "vagrants" of Elizabethan England became the hate-objects of the establishment that "welfare-scroungers" are today, blamed without qualification for their own fate (Bindoff 1950, Ribton-Turner 1887). And the solution proposed by the Elizabethan Poor

Law was precisely that proposed by establishment experts for third world agricultural countries such as Ethiopia encountering the beginning of capitalism today; that the "vagrants" should go back to their own villages and try again, or be relieved there. "Vagrancy" was seen not as the effect, but as the cause of the economic crisis.

This crisis gave rise to a general phenomenon of xenophobic national, ethnic and religious scapegoating. In England the prolonged wars with Spain turned piracy into high patriotism. But it is impossible to displace discontent at home into commitment to foreign wars without at the same time stimulating hatred of the foreigners in our midst. The Jews officially did not exist legally in England, but in the tolerance (or lawlessness, as Tudor apologists would have us call it) of the late middle ages the anti-Jewish laws had become a dead letter. Elizabeth I, however, like Stalin, discovered a Jewish doctors' plot against herself and revived the laws expelling Jews (Pollins 1982). Repatriation of tiny Black communities of retired sailors or freed/abandoned slaves was commenced. Even those immigrant ethnic communities in favour at court, the French and Dutch Protestant refugees, were still the object of popular racism, rioting and discrimination (Holmes 1988, 6-7).

Who then was blamed for the distress and discontent of the later Tudor period? It was foreigners and vagrants. And Gypsies were both. And when the English sought to expel them, they could not, for most neighbouring states were doing likewise.

When Gypsies first reached Western Europe we can see from the sources quoted by economic historians like Jusserand (1888) that commercial nomadism was a vibrant and accepted sector of the medieval economy. Ethnic groups could compete in this on equal terms, as did Travellers from Ireland in other European countries (Acton 1974, 66). The demonisation of vagrancy changed all that, made all Travellers suspect, able to survive only if at every stage of their commercial circuit they could find trusted customers and protectors/patrons – often the very rural magistrates officially required to expel or exterminate them. Sometimes in

England, like the Boswells, they even took the names of their gentry patrons. Commercial nomads of whatever ethnicity had to hang together, or hang separately. And so we find emerging, from the 17th century, in every political unit of north-western Europe, a single, small, localised commercial nomadic group, which, even if it is Romani-identifying, is usually highly adapted to the majority culture of that political unit. Within the British Isles we have four such "old" Travelling groups – the Welsh, English, Scottish and Irish Travellers, that is, in their own languages, the Kale, Romanichals, Nawkens and Minceirs. And there is only ever one group per 16th century political unit, even if there is some territorially-linked linguistic or cultural diversity within the group, as among Scottish Travellers.

It may be true as Kenrick (1989) and Meyer (1891) suggest, as against Macalister, that the phonology of the Gammon language of Irish Travellers indicates that the backslang Irish elements were formed from Middle Irish before ever there were any Romani immigrants in Western Europe. Fair enough. If we want to think of the Romanichals as an essentially Gypsy group who absorbed a number of local English Travellers and customs, and of the Irish Travellers as an essentially Irish group who must have absorbed whichever few Romani immigrants reached 16th century Ireland (along with their cleanliness taboo system), and naturally enough wanted to differentiate themselves sharply from the genocidal violence the English were liable to inflict on those labelled "Egyptians" or "pretended Egyptians" wherever they extended their sphere of influence in the 17th century: if we want to understand the groups' historical identity in this way, then what harm does it do anybody?

The harm that it does is to divert attention away from the processes by which the contemporary identity of Western Europe's Travelling groups were formed. We have to accept that neither the Romani people(s), nor the richly textured native European commercial nomadism revealed by Jusserand (1888), exist today as they existed in 1500. In the persecutions of the 16th century, the previous identities of Europe's Travelling groups are broken and re-moulded into something new – and in a sense, whether that new identity is Romani-identifying or not is an accident of history. Irish Travellers, like other Traveller groups, are what they are, and nothing else (or, in potential, of course, everything else). When we are persistently asked "But who are the Irish Travellers, actually", the correct response is neither to answer the question like Kenrick, or to ignore it like Okely, but to deconstruct the necessity of defining any group's identity in terms of some other group's identity; which for Travellers is inevitably to expose the burying of the knowledge in Western Europe about what was actually done to Travellers, the forgotten genocide at the heart of the European unconscious.

When the Rom of Eastern Europe face Travellers of Western Europe, it is the survivors of slavery facing the survivors of genocide. This is not to say that all Rom were slaves, any more than all Romanichals or Sinte were commercial nomads; but slavery and genocide were the differing keys to the catastrophe wrought among Gypsies in East and West in 16th century Europe. As from the 19th century there was renewed international migration of Gypsies, the survivors of slavery and the survivors of genocide faced a common fate in the renewed anti-Gypsy and anti-Traveller persecutions and genocides of the 20th century. If these groups wish to reach a common strategy to resist this, the first requirement is a mutual and compassionate understanding of each others' different histories, one that will not sweep aside the traumatising effects of these histories as shameful. It is for this reason that the exploration by Romani intellectuals like Hancock (1987) and Maximoff (1946, 1981) on the effects of persecution is so important a constituent factor of contemporary Gypsy politics.

But we must also insist that it is equally important for non-Gypsies, for *buffers*. If we ever do wish to build the common European home on a basis of truth and justice and respect for all, we need first of all to take the common European skeleton out of the common European cupboard, to free ourselves from the racist myths which taint the construction of all our national and ethnic identities, and not only those of Travellers.

REFERENCES

Acton, T.

Gypsy Politics and Social Change. London: Routledge & Kegan Paul, 1974.

"The Social Construction of the Ethnic Identity of Commercial Nomadic Groups", *Papers from the 4th and 5th Annual Meetings of the Gypsy Lore Society North American Chapter*, G. L. S. J. Grumet (ed.). New York, 1985.

"Oppositions Theoriques entre Tsiganologues, et Distinctions entre Groupes Tsiganes", in Williams, 1989.

"The Social Construction and Consequences of Accusations of False Claims to Ethnicity and Cultural Rights", *Paper to Leiden University Foundation Centennial Conference*, September, 1990.

"Defining the Limits of Tolerance: UK Government Policy on Gypsies", *Paper to the Lacio Drom Conference*. Rome, September, 1991.

Arnold, H.

"The Gypsy Gene", *Journal of the Gypsy Lore Society*, III series, 40, 1961, 53-6.

Randgruppen des Zigeunervolkes, Neustadt Weinstrasse: Pfälzische Verlagsanstalt, 1975.

Bakker, P. and M. Cortiade

In the Margin of Romani: Gypsy Languages in Contact. University of Amsterdam Institute for General Linguistics. Studies in Language Contact, Vol. 1, 1991.

Bindoff, S.T.

Tudor England. Harmondsworth: Penguin, 1950.

Black, G. F.

A Gypsy Bibliography. London: T.A. Constable for the Gypsy Lore Society, 1913.

Clark, G. and D. Todd

Gypsy Site Provision and Policy. London: Department of the Environment/H.M.S.O., 1991a.

	Good Practice Guidelines for Gypsy Site Provision. London: Department of the Environment/H.M.S.O., 1991b.
Cortiade, M.	"Romani versus Para-Romani", in *Bakker and Cortiade*, 1991.
Crawford, M.H.	"Genetic Affinities and Origins of the Irish Tinkers", in *Biosocial Interrelations in Population Adaptation*. E. S. Watts, F. E. Johnston and G.W. Lasker (eds.), The Hague: Mouton, 1975.
Dodds, N.	*Gypsies, Didikois and Other Travellers*. London: Johnson, 1966.
Green, H.	*Counting Gypsies*. London: Department of the Environment/ H.M.S.O., 1991.
Hancock, I. F.	"Romani and Angloromani" and "Shelta and Polari", in *Language in the British Isles*. P. Trudgill (ed.). London: Cambridge University Press, 1984.
	The Pariah Syndrome. Ann Arbor, Mich.: Karoma, 1987.
	"The Development of Romani Linguistics", *Jazyery and Winter*. 1988, 183-223.
	"The Romani Speech Community", in *Multi-Lingualism in the British Isles*, Vol. 1. S. Alladina & V. Edwards (eds.). London: Longman, 1991.
Holmes, C.	*John Bull's Island*. Basingstoke: Macmillan, 1988.
Jazyery, A. and W. Winter (eds.)	*Papers in honour of Edgar C. Polome*. The Hague: Mouton, 1988.
Jusserand, J. J.	*English Wayfaring Life in the Middle Ages*. Williamstown MA: Corner House, 1888, repr. 1974.
Kenrick, D.	"How Old is Shelta?", *Romani Institute Occasional Paper* No. 2, 1989.

Kenrick, D. and Bakewell, S.	*On the Verge: The Gypsies of England.* London: Runnymede Trust, 1990.
Liégeois, J-P.	*Gypsies and Travellers.* Strasbourg: Council of Europe, 1987.
Macalister, R.A.S.	*The Secret Languages of Ireland.* Cambridge: Cambridge University Press, 1937.
MacRitchie, D.	*Scottish Gypsies under the Stewarts.* Edinburgh: D. Douglas, 1894.
Maximoff, M.	"Germany and the Gypsies", *Journal of the Gypsy Lore Society,* Series III, 25 (3-4), 1946.
	Le Prix de la Liberté, 2nd Ed. Paris: Concordia, 1981.
Mayall, D.	"Defining the Gypsy : Ethnicity, 'Race' and Representation". *Paper to Leiden University Foundation Centennial Conference.* September, 1990.
Meyer, K.	"The Irish Origin and the Age of Shelta", *Journal of the Gypsy Lore Society,* Series I, 2, 1891, 257.
Ní Shúinéar, S.	"The Irish Travellers: 'Solving' an Ethnic Minority", with subsequently circulated postscript, *Paper to Leiden University Foundation Centennial Conference,* September, 1990.
Odley, T.	Private Correspondence, 1984, quoted in Searchlight, March 1989, 8, "Racial Romany Gets Left-wing Platform" and in Acton 1991.
Okely, J.	*The Traveller Gypsies.* London: Cambridge University Press. 1983.
Papp, G.	A Beás Cigányok Román Nyelvjárása, Janus Pannonius University Pedagogical Department Gypsy Research Series Vol V, Pecs, Hungary, 1982.
Pollins, H.	*Economic History of the Jews in England.* London & Toronto: Associated University Presses, 1982.

Rao, A. (ed.)   *The Other Nomads: Peripatetic Minorities in Cross-Cultural Perspective.* Cologne and Vienna: Bölau Verlag, 1987.

Ribton-Turner, C. J.   *A History of Vagrants and Vagrancy.* Montclair NJ: Patterson Smith, 1887, repr. 1972.

Tawney, R.H.   *The Agrarian Problem in the Sixteenth Century.* London: Longmans, 1912.

Tawney, R.H. (with E. Power)   *Tudor Economic Documents.* London: Longmans, 1924.

Vaux de Foletier, F. de   *Mille Ans d'Histoire des Tsiganes.* Paris: Fayard, 1970.

Vesey-Fitzgerald, F.   *Gypsies of Britain,* New Enlarged Edition. Newton Abbot: David and Charles, 1973.

Williams, E.Mair   "Genetic Studies of Welsh Gypsies", in *Genetic and Population Studies in Wales.* P. S. Harper and E. Sunderland. Cardiff: University of Wales Press, 1986.

Williams, P. (ed.)   *Tsiganes: Identité, Evolution.* Paris: Syros, 1989.

IRISH TRAVELLERS, ETHNICITY AND THE ORIGINS QUESTION

Sinéad Ní Shúinéar

*still is
is an
later*

In recent years, ethnicity has been one of the most debated topics in relation to Travellers in Ireland, with passionate debate over whether it applies: whether Irish Travellers are a distinct ethnic group and what follows from this. This debate has also raised the question of the origins of Irish Travellers. In this chapter I argue that Irish Travellers meet all the objective scientific criteria of an ethnic group. I then discuss some of the issues that arise in the study of the history of Irish Travellers. I conclude with some brief comments on the politics of debates on ethnicity and origins.

IRISH TRAVELLERS AND ETHNICITY

According to the anthropologist F. Barth (1970):

"The term 'ethnic group' is generally understood in anthropological literature to designate a population which is biologically self-perpetuating, shares fundamental cultural values realised in overt unity of cultural form, makes up a field of communication and interaction, and has a population which defines itself, and is defined by others, as constituting a category distinguishable from other categories of the same order . . . The itemised characteristics imply: racial difference, cultural difference, social separation, language barriers, and spontaneous and organised enmity."

Barth himself dissents from this concept of ethnicity in favour of a more transactional approach.

Do Irish Travellers constitute a distinct ethnic group? To answer this question we look at Irish Travellers from the standpoint of this definition. The first criterion is *biological self-perpetuation* and the basic requirement here is that, on the whole, people marry within the group. This is certainly true of Irish Travellers the vast majority of whom marry other Travellers. Marriage for Travellers is more a socio-political alliance than a personal whim, and has profound implications for group membership: the one absolutely decisive factor in whether an individual is a Traveller or not is whether he has at least one Traveller parent.

An implication of this first criterion is *racial difference*. Physical distinctiveness in the broadest sense is not synonymous with identity, but intra-marriage tends to keep the two pretty closely linked. Travellers are physically distinctive from the settled[1] population. Ask any Traveller who, scrubbed and combed and decked out in all new gear, has been refused entry to a pub or disco without even getting a chance to open his mouth, and you will find that physical distinctiveness not only exists, but exists in very practical ways. Ask any bouncer or security guard and you'll get the same answer. Genetic studies corroborate this popular perception by confirming differentiation between the Traveller and settled Irish populations (Crawford and Gmelch 1974; Crawford 1976).

Irish Travellers also meet the criterion of *shared fundamental cultural values* and its concomitant *cultural difference*. The core values of Irish Travellers include: self-employment, occupational flexibility, priority of social obligations based on kinship over everything else, nomadism as a functional corollary of the above and as a value in itself, strict segregation of pure and impure, versatility, adaptability, and skill in the delicate art of living among and supplying the market demands of the non-Traveller majority, without losing their Traveller identity.

Limitations of space permit me to focus on just one of these values, one perhaps unsuspected by most settled observers: Traveller categories of pure and impure, clean and unclean, and the value they place on cleanliness. Okely has analysed these in great detail for English Gypsies; they may be also observed among Irish Travellers. Thus items deemed to be polluted are instantly discarded without regard to cost or inconvenience. Every Traveller home has a series of basins, each of which is used exclusively for a given category of washing: delft in one, clothing in another, floorcloths in another, the body in another. Pollution occurs when items from one category cross over into another: for example, if a cup were to be washed in the basin meant for hands, or a teatowel (always washed in the delft basin) to get mixed in with the dirty clothes.

Settled observers see Traveller homes from the outside – the surrounding squalor – and jump to the conclusion that the interiors are the same; when and if they do get an inside glimpse of the gleaming china and mirrors they are invariably astonished. Part of the misunderstanding stems from the two groups' different attitudes towards "ownership" of space. Traveller and settled people share two of these: home as the inner sanctuary, to be kept immaculate, and the world at large which is somebody else's responsibility and which both groups are by and large shameless about polluting. The point is that while no one would stub a cigarette underfoot in their own kitchen, everybody does so at bus stops: different standards apply. The misunderstanding arises because settled people recognise a third category separating the two with an ambiguous area around the home, which is in some ways an extension of it (people take enormous pride in their front gardens) and in others a no-man's land (most people's sheds are not quite as tidy as their sitting rooms). Travellers by contrast – in common with all nomadic peoples – do not feel any personal responsibility for the area around the home. It is, if you like, a sort of bus stop and this gives rise to very real tension between the two communities.

Travellers also meet the third criterion of ethnic group identity, *overt unity of cultural form* and the *social separation* implied. "Cultural form" covers a multitude of observable phenomena: accommodation, dress and grooming, speech patterns, group rituals such as religious ceremonies and funerals, and artistic expression. Traveller versions of all of these are distinctive – identifiably Traveller; that is how and why Travellers are "different". A unity of form does not of course mean everyone is identical; it just means that there is more in common than not, and this is recognisable to the outside observer.

Travellers also operate within their own *field of communication and interaction.* While the Traveller has dealings with settled people when selling carpets, collecting scrap, and begging, as well as in connection with hospitals, schools, religious duties, social welfare, and the courts, all of these dealings are purposeful: they are not social calls. Travellers and settled people meet head-on rather than side-by-side; they do not work or drink or live or play or go to school together. The settled community is very anxious indeed to keep Travellers well out of its "field of communication and interaction". The RTE television drama series Glenroe has shown Travellers attempting to book a hotel for a wedding reception through a settled intermediary, only to have the booking cancelled when their identity became known; they were subsequently offered the use of the church hall by a kindly priest, where they would be "out of the way". In fact these are scenes from real life, where one also finds Traveller children segregated into "special classes" in isolated prefabs with separate play-times. It is also the common experience of Travellers, when not denied access outright to shops, to find themselves followed, in heavy-handed efforts to discourage shop-lifting. Travellers maintain the barriers with more subtle methods, notably by overwhelming with requests the settled person who gets too close: the more urgently the Traveller implores the country person to approach, the more rapidly the latter will back away.

We come to the fourth implication of ethnic distinctiveness – the presence of *language barriers.* Since language is covered elsewhere in this volume (Binchy Ch.10), I will deal with it in a series of very broad points. Language barriers between the Travelling and settled populations are twofold. The first of these, rarely accorded any serious consideration, is Travellers' use of English. This is so distinctive that "uninitiated" settled people often have difficulty understanding

Travellers' speech even when Travellers are trying their best to be understood. Traveller English is a cohesive entity, spoken by all Irish Travellers regardless of geography; the Traveller who has spent most of his life around Cork speaks essentially the same dialect as the Traveller who has spent most of his life in Dublin, Belfast, Galway or for that matter London, despite the enormous variations displayed by the settled speakers by whom they are surrounded and with whom they interact. Traveller English is a cohesive and distinctive entity because of its Gammon underlay.[2]

This brings us to Travellers' own language, Gammon or Cant. The conventional wisdom is that Travellers' language is a kind of schoolboys' backslang deliberately made up out of bits of scrambled Irish in order to conceal skulduggery from decent settled folk. This is a hypothesis which has never been systematically investigated, but is nonetheless treated as fact. It ignores much contrary evidence. First, Gammon forms the syntactical underlay of Traveller English, as mentioned above. Second, this view ignores the tenacity of Gammon,which has proven a lot more tenacious than the Irish language for the general population. It is spoken not only by all Irish Travellers both here and in Britain, but also by the descendants of Irish Travellers who emigrated to the U.S. over a century and a half ago, and have not retained contact with Travellers here. This also begs the intriguing question as to why Irish Traveller emigrants have hung on to Gammon, while settled Irish emigrants have not held on to Irish, and why, if the whole *raison d'être* of Gammon is concealing communication, Irish Travellers chose to hold onto it, rather than to Irish, the "real" language, a language at least as incomprehensible to the American settled population as Gammon. Third, this view ignores the historical evidence of monolingual (Gammon only) Travellers (Macalister 1937, 136).

Fourth, it ignores its use in the home. Traveller children learn Gammon from the cradle. No parent would deliberately teach a two-year-old a dual vocabulary with the proviso that some words are "secret". Fifth, it ignores the existence of words that are for internal consumption only, as pointed out by Dr. Anthony Cash, a Traveller linguist and native speaker of Gammon (Cash 1977). Sixth, it is simply not feasible that a fragmented, nomadic people, having very little contact with each other but a great deal with the settled population from whom they supposedly derive, could devise and pool a common linguistic heritage so pervasive that it colours their use of a second language, English. Finally, the devices by which it is claimed that Irish was "scrambled" into Gammon are both arbitrary and far-fetched (Ní Shúinear 1979). It is true that a very limited number of Gammon words can be turned into their Irish equivalents by swapping syllables around, but what about the rest of the language?

Finally, Travellers also meet the fifth criterion of ethnicity: *self ascription ("a membership which defines itself") and outside ascription ("is defined by others")*: Travellers have a name for themselves as a group, and they know exactly who does and does not belong to it, and why. Non-Travellers also have names for Travellers as a group, and they too know exactly to whom they apply and (by criteria which are very different from Travellers' own) why. It is worth noting that settled perceptions of Travellers are so overpoweringly negative that if the individual Traveller demonstrates that he or she clearly does not conform to the negative stereotypes, he or she is suddenly redeemed from Traveller status: they become "a former itinerant", "a housed Traveller", "a settled Traveller" "of Traveller stock" or whatever.[3] Travellers also have their own terms for non-Travellers. The most emotionally neutral of these, "country people", is, if one stops to think about it, an extraordinary term for one rural people to apply to another.

The final implication is *spontaneous and organised enmity*. We need look no further than our daily papers for examples of this: from the more dramatic manifestations like pickets, marches and mob attacks on Traveller camps, to the institutionalised harassment of evictions and the deliberate blocking off and destruction of any and all possible camp sites by boulders (officially termed "landscaping"), to the *de facto* apartheid of barring Travellers from pubs, schools, and dances on the (all too often justified) grounds that their presence would lead to "trouble".

In short, we are dealing with a group that fulfils all the objective scientific criteria to qualify as an ethnic group.

THE QUESTION OF ORIGINS

Tracing the history of all nomadic peoples is notoriously difficult. First, and most obvious, nomadism means a material culture pared down to the portable minimum: a surfeit of possessions would quite literally tie the nomad down. It also means little or no traces left of one's passing. 40,000 years of Aboriginal life have left Australian archaeologists nothing to work on but a handful of rock paintings, and even these – unlike, say, irrigation networks or pottery – are virtually meaningless without inside explanation.

Second, some nomadic peoples – the Jews of the Old Testament spring immediately to mind – cultivate both literacy and historical memory. Others, even without literacy, enshrine genealogy and significant events into formal litanies to be memorised and passed on verbatim by specialists. But others still – and this includes most commercial nomadic groups – treat the past itself as a sort of baggage, a surfeit of which would tie them down in the present. Instead, they cultivate an intense present-time orientation, living in a perpetual now, deriving their sense of identity not from taproots deep into the past, but from vast networks of living kin. The essence of Gypsy and Traveller culture is its fluidity.[4]

Gypsies and Travellers everywhere are supremely indifferent to their own origins. Some groups have charming legends, either for internal consumption or for gullible outsiders: for example, the famous story of the smith who made the nails for Jesus's crucifixion being condemned to wander, or the wonderful fantasy about being Egyptian nobles on prolonged pilgrimage. There is no hard core of sober fact under all this, though; no tribal *seanachie* with the inside track on who begat whom. Quite the contrary: it wasn't until the mid-19th century that a Hungarian pastor identified the linguistic – and thus historical and racial – links between Romani and the languages of India. The Romani speakers themselves knew and cared nothing for this fascinating snippet, and by and large this continues to hold true even today.

Given that the two most obvious sources, archaeological evidence and internal records written or oral, do not apply here, we are left with the written and oral records of outside observers for hard chronology, and with other, more subtle, sources of an ethnographic and linguistic nature.

The records of outside observers present many problems. Such sources – written often with an eye fiercely jaundiced – frequently tell us more about the attitudes and reactions of the observers than about the observed. Whatever the accuracy of their content, they do serve to establish hard chronology; we can trace the arrival and migrations of the first Romanis in Europe through the trail of repressive legislation which sprang up in their wake. Yet even this is not free of ambiguity: despite the racial distinctiveness of Romani immigrants – Travelling People of Indian origin – writers do not always clearly identify the group with a unique label such as "Egyptians". For example, in Elizabethan times, the popular descriptive term applied to them was simply "rogues" (Mayall 1990, 4).

Bearing all of this in mind, let us turn to the Irish situation. Travellers here are not racially striking, nor did they arrive suddenly from abroad, nor did they propagate any fabulous claims as to who they were; they nonetheless evoked as much hostility as their darker-skinned counterparts. Historical references to Irish Travellers are beset by all the complications pertaining to Gypsies (as outlined above) and more. In particular, one can never be certain that a given reference – particularly the very early ones – really does refer to Irish Travellers, who then as now are sometimes (and erroneously) classified as an occupational group ("tinsmiths", "whitesmiths"), sometimes as a social category ("vagabonds", "wild Irishmen").

To date, very little serious research into even the most obvious historical source materials, and virtually none in related fields such as toponymy, has been done in relation to Irish Travellers. Even so, a clear thread leads us back to the distant past:

"As early as pre-Christian times (5th c. and earlier), itinerant whitesmiths working in bronze, gold and silver travelled the Irish countryside making personal ornaments, weapons and horse-trappings in exchange for food and lodging" (Gmelch and Gmelch 1976, 227).

"By 1175, 'tinkler' and 'tynker' began appearing in records as trade or surnames; by 1300 they were common" (Gmelch and Gmelch 1976, 227).

"In 1243, an English law was passed, aimed at curtailing the 'wandering Irish', another in 1413 under Henry V, and another 9 years later, in 1422, under Henry VI" (Kenrick 1979, 1).

Historian David Mayall, outlining 16th-18th century sources on Gypsies in England, notes:

"The term 'Egyptian' was the first known classification for the group of people later referred to as gypsies . . . and was subsequently used as a defining label for gypsies and non-gypsies alike" (Mayall 1990, 5).

This foreign designation was a protective loophole for 'rogues and vagabonds' born within the British Isles;

"The legislative solution was to amend the provisions . . . to include persons disguised as Egyptians or who were consorting with Egyptians, and to describe them as 'counterfayte Egyptians'" (Mayall 1990, 5)·

Learning that this group had – skin colour aside – so much in common with Romani Gypsies, tells us a great deal.

Historically, various terms coexist side by side, just as to-day one encounters a range of designations ranging from "roadside traders" to "dealers" to "knackers"; the predominant, recurring term is the familiar "tinker". Still in the 16th century, we have a Shakespearean reference: in *Henry IV* (2.4) Prince Hal boasts of being able to "drink with any tinker in his own language". In 1552, King Edward VI passed an "Acte for tynkers and pedlers":

"... *no person or persons commonly called tynker, pedler, or pety chapman shall wander or go from one towne to another or from place to place out of the towne, parish or village ...*" (Gmelch and Gmelch 1976, 228).

"*By the 16th century it appears than 'tinkers' (...) were well-established in both Ireland and Scotland. Several writers have attributed the failure of Gypsies, who were also metal workers, to become established in either country at this time as due to the stiff competition they met from native tinkers*" (Gmelch and Gmelch 1976, 227)·

"*In the Elizabethan references, there are distinctions made between 'tinkers' and Egipcyans (sic), and yet they are often included together, as a group*" (O'Toole, 58).

In 1619, Thomas Gainsford, a soldier in the Irish Wars, noted the widespread existence of "gravers in gold and silver called plain tinkers" (Gmelch and Gmelch 1976, 227). The Journal of the Gypsy Lore Society reproduced "a true inventory of all ye goods credits and chattels of Nicholas Leigh a Tinker-errant ... taken the 15th day of September anno domini 1632" (Gypsy Lore Soc. Jnl. 1977, 177).

"*In the literature of 17th, 18th and 19th century Scotland and England there are many interchangeable references to Gypsies and 'tinkers' ... There are many historical and literary references to tinkers in all parts of the British Isles. The first Stewarts, especially James I of Scotland, are legendary in their relations with them. There is also much evidence that the Scottish 'tinkers' moved back and forth from Ireland to the Highlands and Islands in the Western Channel, inter-marrying for many centuries ... not only are there accounts of marriages, but in some of the islands off the coast of Scotland pointing to Ireland ... there are references to largely Shelta-speaking people*" (O'Toole, 57-58).

Once into the 17th century, written sources become ever clearer, and more numerous. They are also, thanks to the

Irish Traveller Resource Collection housed at the University of Ulster at Jordanstown[5], easily accessible. The earliest source in the collection is the account books of a County Antrim vicar (kept from 1672-1680) containing frequent references to "tinklars" or "tinkers", and of transactions with them; for example he describes the annual visits of a family group to the rectory, begging food and clothing, and mentions the women as being strikingly distinct from the general population, with very dark hair and eyes and brightly coloured plaid skirts.

Reading through three centuries of references compiled in these volumes, one is overwhelmed with a sense of *déjà vu*; references to "sharp" business practices, falsehood, general lawlessness and even "unnatural powers" occur with monotonous regularity – as does counter-propaganda, assertions of a "carefree, colourful existence", the "noble life of the open road".

Popular speculation as to their origin includes Phoenician tinsmiths, the Lapps, a "prehistoric guild of bronzeworkers", armourers to the ancient kings of Ireland, the "dregs of an aboriginal people", Famine victims, pre-Celtic goldworkers, victims of Cromwell, able-bodied voluntary beggars, Picts, tinsmiths who gradually evolved a separate identity and so on. The tinsmithing angle is particularly enlightening. Virtually all the sources treat "tinker" (ethnic category) and "tinsmith" (occupational category) as synonymous, yet trading in horses and donkeys is mentioned just as often as tinsmithing. Indeed the collected sources give us an invaluable overview of the occupational fluidity typical of Travellers (and this characteristic is itself mentioned by two of the sources) as well as putting the diversity into historical perspective. Mention is made of begging, hawking/peddling, fortune-telling, *poitín*-making, repairing of china, skilled metalwork, selling feathers, making and hawking paper flowers, work in the construction industry, soldiering, fruitselling, harvesting, music, scrap, trading in goats' meat, cattle-dealing, car and lorry dealing, shop-keeping, rags, bottles, horsehair, chimneysweeping, and "Gypsying" (as an occupation?). I might add that even this seemingly exhaustive list omits several occupations commonly practised by Travellers today: carpet, linoleum, and furniture dealing, tarmac'ing, antiques.

Valuable information of an historical and linguistic kind will also be found in contemporary research on Irish Traveller communities in the U.S. These are descended from Travellers who emigrated at the time of the Famine, and who have not maintained contact with Travellers in Ireland. Since both groups have been evolving separately for a century and a half now, it is clear that whatever is both unique and common to the two must have existed before the split.

Anthropological study of Irish Travellers in the U.S. has been carried on largely by Jared Harper of the University of Georgia, who has concentrated on, but not limited himself to, a study of their language. The community he has studied comprises some 1,200 individuals. Here are some brief extracts describing this community in 1971: "According to Traveler tradition, they emigrated from Ireland about 1847, around the time of the Irish Potato Famine . . . Upon their arrival in America, so the Travelers say, the immigrants settled first in upstate New York, near Buffalo; near Pittsburgh and Germanstown, Pennsylvania; and near Washington D.C. . . . About the time of the American Civil War, my informants state, they abandoned all other occupations and moved to the south, and specialised in the mule and horse trade until about 1955 when that trade virtually ceased . . . As a rule only the men travel today, while the women and children remain at home in modern house trailers . . . Since the demise of the mule trade the Travelers have devised two new itinerant occupational specialities: peddling linoleum rugs door-to-door and spray painting barns and houses . . . adopting as fulltime employment what was once only a summer diversion from the normal routine of mule trading." Dr. Harper gives a "rough estimate" of a total of 5000 IrishTravellers living "in several permanent and semi-permanent communities in Georgia, South Carolina, Mississippi, Louisiana, Texas and Tennessee" (Harper 1971, 18-19).

But it is the language on which scholars have focused. Dr. Harper collected about 250 phrases and sentences, and reckons the average vocabulary of Travellers in the 35+ age group at about 150 words, with the younger generation knowing just half as many. I recently received, from Dr. Ian Hancock, the Gypsy linguist at the University of Austin, Texas, a list of 300 words collected from Irish Travellers in Texas in 1984. I presented this list, word by word, to a group of half a dozen middle-aged Travelling women in Dublin. They recognised 83 of them – well over a quarter. This offers at once empirical proof of the linguistic continuity between Irish Travellers in the U.S. and Ireland, and evidence that Irish Travellers – with their characteristic economic base, nomadism, language, and consciousness of "country people" as separate – were well established by that date. We might also ask why, given the opportunity to start afresh in the New World and lose their pariah status, Irish Travellers did not do so: the most efficient "melting pot" in the world has failed to dissolve their distinctiveness.

TRAVELLER ORIGINS:
THE CONVENTIONAL WISDOM

Conventional wisdom insists that Irish Travellers are essentially dropouts from normal society, victims of their own inadequacy or of harsh colonialism, and a relatively new phenomenon, dating back to the Famine or at most to Cromwell. This view is passionately, almost universally, held, and would not merit serious consideration but for its extremely serious implications for settled attitudes – and therefore policies – towards Travellers. It is open to objection on several grounds.

One argument offered in support of it claims that many aspects of the Traveller way of life are similar to those of the Irish peasantry in Famine times. Travellers are thus dispossessed peasants with a timelag, clinging to customs which the rest of us outgrew long ago, such as arranged marriages, clans, large numbers of children, an attachment to horses. This argument is both ethnocentric and one-sided. It is ethnocentric because it assumes that the items mentioned are unique to Irish folk culture and could therefore only have come from it. It is one-sided because it ignores those aspects of Irish Traveller culture which are not shared with the peasantry. It also ignores those elements which are radically opposed: the rejection of land ownership, of sedentarism itself, of a "steady job", the significant differences between the ways the two communities practice their (ostensibly shared) religion, the opposing concepts of cleanliness which give rise to so much tension between the two.

Another argument stresses that Traveller surnames are Irish. This argument is also problematic. Travellers, Irish or otherwise, have a rather fluid relationship to names generally, and Travelling People all over the world bear names which resemble those of surrounding society: Lee and Penfold are archetypally English Gypsy names, but do not occur in France, Germany, or Sweden. But, the argument goes on, these aren't just *any* Irish surnames. They are surnames from the West of Ireland, the region where the peasantry – the McDonaghs, Wards and Joyces – was hardest hit by famine, eviction, and general economic hardship. The predominance of names from the worst-affected areas appears to support the view that Travellers are the descendants of dispossessed peasants from these areas. However this argument, too, is incomplete. The most typical West of Ireland surnames – such as Flaherty, Conneely, Naughton – do not appear among Travellers at all. Moreover, many typical Traveller surnames, such as, for example, Mongans, do not appear among the settled population at all. As a matter of fact, the 1963 Report found that a mere 9 surnames accounted for 35.64% of the Traveller population. Are we to believe that all of the Mongans "took to the road", while none of the Flahertys or Naughtons did?

A third argument holds that the Travelling population is riddled with social problems – alcoholism, criminality, chronic unemployment – and that this indicates that they are the descendants of problem-ridden persons who had to drop out of society because they were unable to cope with it; these problems have then been passed on to subsequent generations. This is a very superficial view, easily refuted. Traveller deviants are highly visible, and biased media ensure that the

Traveller identity of a given criminal, or even suspect, is emphasised. Statistics tell a different story: the incidence of alcoholism among Travellers is in fact somewhat lower than among the general population, and Traveller criminality is on the whole of a petty, non-violent nature – petty indeed, considering that their whole way of life, their horses, their "temporary dwellings", have been criminalised. As for chronic unemployment: Travellers are not *un-*employed, they are *self-*employed. They don't surround themselves with scrap because they like squalor, but because there's money in it.

The above hypothesis – which I have termed "the drop-out theory" – is mere conventional wisdom, which was lent a spurious air of academic legitimacy through being uncritically accepted, and reiterated, by the American anthropologists George and Sharon Gmelch. "Tinkers", they state, are descended from ". . . sedentary Irish . . . forced to adopt a nomadic existence . . . Peasants and laborers were forced to become itinerant as the result of widespread evictions, unemployment, and famine" (Gmelch and Gmelch 1976, 225). "Personal problems, such as illegitimacy or alcoholism, sometimes forced an individual or family into itinerancy. The literature contains numerous references to 'strolling women' – women stigmatised and driven to begging and sometimes prostitution because of illegitimate children" (Gmelch 1977, 10).

This view is simply *post hoc* reasoning, retrospective justification for a faulty premise, and can be summarised as "Today's Travellers are social deviants; therefore, they must be descended from social deviants". It postulates that problem families, individual winos, and prostitutes, thrown together at the margins of society, somehow developed a shared identity, gradually evolving into today's Travellers. Such a view ignores two crucial facts. First, that "the side of the road" was not a sociocultural *tabula rasa*: historical references confirm Travellers' existence from at least the 13th century onwards. These drop-outs would thus have been required to assimilate into an alien culture and society despite their inability to cope with the one they were born into. Second, the argument assumes that assimilation into Traveller identity is possible, but this is not so. No one can *become* a Traveller; membership is determined by birth into the group, and Traveller identity is intensely bound up in labyrinthine webs of kinship.

It is true that settled dropouts who adopted nomadism would have increased opportunity for contact with, and therefore increased potential for marriage into, the group. Yet such a hypothesis presupposes consensual unions, whereas Traveller marriages are arranged, between kin, in early puberty. At any rate, the children of such mixed unions would, *if raised as Travellers*, be accepted as Travellers; the settled partner never is. Recognising the possibility of gradual assimilation of the children of mixed marriages into a preexisting sociocultural entity – ethnic group – is a far cry from postulating that settled dropouts created it, or at least numerically swamped whatever core group there may have been.

In fact historical references state unequivocally that even at the times of greatest hardship amongst the settled population, forcing them into itinerancy and begging, these persons did not assimilate into the Travelling community:

"*In 1834, the Royal Commission on the Poor Laws estimated that there were 2,358,000 beggars and their dependents (almost one-third of the total population) on the roads of Ireland at least part of the year. Of these, tinker families formed a distinct and recognisable group. A resident of County Longford told the Commission on the Condition of the Poorer Classes: "Ordinary beggars do not become a separate class of the community, but wandering tinkers, families who always beg, do. Three generations of them have been seen begging together." That was written in 1835, as were the following words from Co. Mayo: "The wives and families accompany the tinker while he strolls about in search of work, and always beg. They inter-marry with one another, and form a distinct class*" (quoted Gmelch and Gmelch 1976, 228).

Dr. Gmelch nonetheless goes on to postulate the gradual development of "a separate identity . . . based on similarity of life-styles". However, while motorisation has meant vastly increased mobility, most nomadic Travellers continue to cover a fairly restricted, and regular, circuit. Until forced into high-concentration urban ghettos, they always camped in very small groups. Weddings and funerals bring together large numbers of people who are already related, but not outsiders. In fact, Travellers meet in very large numbers, from very wide distances, only at a small number of annual fairs. This means that not only were they not meeting each other, but, until they acquired their own mobile shelter around the beginning of the 19th century, they were interacting frequently with the very people from whom they supposedly derive (being sheltered in their homes and outbuildings). The advent of the tent, and later the caravan, meant decreased interaction with non-Travellers, but this does not imply a compensatory increase of interaction between Travellers. Even today, factional hostility between Travellers is rife, and Travellers try to avoid contact with members of rival clans; when lumped together indiscriminately in local authority provision, mistrust turns to open conflict.

In fact all the evidence challenges the view that a motley collection of dispossessed peasants, alcoholics, prostitutes and general misfits could ever have evolved into the coherent ethnic group we examined earlier.

TRAVELLER ORIGIN: THREE HYPOTHESES

If Irish Travellers did not originate in the way the conventional wisdom assumes, where did they come from? This is a question for historians and linguists, not anthropologists. I can, however, suggest a couple of alternative hypotheses as guidelines for them, while stressing that I am not proposing any of these as a new conventional wisdom to replace the old.

Hypothesis One: The Irish Travellers are the descendants of a pre-Celtic group living in Ireland and relegated to inferior status by Celtic invaders. They may or may not have been nomadic at the time of the invasion.

In India the indigenous Dravidic population was relegated to inferior status by Aryan invaders. Status became institutionalised as the caste system, then justified on religious grounds by claiming that the very lowest – those outside the caste system altogether – are in this position because of their occupations, which happen to be those most typically associated with Indian Travellers at home and abroad. For Ireland, no one knows what happened to the Tuatha dé Danann, the Fir Bolg, and all the other pre-Celtic peoples who are mere legends to us. That they retained a distinct identity after conquest – even if enslaved, as Romanian Gypsies were for centuries – is a possibility worth looking into.

Hypothesis Two: The Irish Travellers are the descendants of one of several distinct Celtic groups which invaded Ireland over a period of several centuries.

It is known, for example, that Ulster and Connacht were colonised by entirely different tribes, and that this was reflected in historical enmity between the provinces – as recounted in the *Táin*. Either of these hypotheses would explain the existence of a separate language unique to but shared by all Travellers.

Hypothesis Three: The Irish Travellers are descended from indigenous nomadic craftsmen who never became sedentary – whether these craftsmen were separate from, a distinct subgroup within, or drawn from the Celtic invaders.

Ireland – like every region inhabited by the ancient Celts – has a vast legacy of stunningly wrought metalwork – tools, weapons, jewellery – from long before the Christian era, a time when the Celts were a restless nomadic or semi-nomadic people. Clearly, work of such high quality came not from peasants, but from the hands of skilled, specialised craftsmen. The Celts became more sedentary with the passage of time, but in Ireland lived in very low density settlements. The monasteries, from the 5th century onwards, were the first concentrations of population in Ireland. We may conclude that agricultural methods up until then did not produce sufficient surplus to support large numbers of non-farmers. Yet the skilled metalwork continues through the period, so who was producing it? Is it not reasonable to assume that isolated farmsteads had enough surplus food to barter for individual metal items, but not enough to support such crafts-men fulltime? In this case, the metalworkers would have to remain nomadic in order to find their markets, and, since payment must have been in the form of bulky, perishable foodstuffs, the entire family must have travelled together. The wife and children, freed from the agricultural labour of their sedentary counterparts, would have evolved other ways of contributing to the family economy. Later, under Viking influence, larger population centres did arise, so that crafts-men could sedentarise and have customers come to them. But this did not eliminate market demands arising only sea-sonally or occasionally – for example harvesting, mending, horse trading, entertainment at fairs – and the travelling groups who met them.

CONCLUSION

I want to conclude with a few remarks on the origins controversy itself. Not long ago, I had the honour of partici-pating in a major international conference on minority rights[6]. To my amazement, the Gypsy and Traveller section of the conference was rent with the same impassioned debate on origins as we have witnessed here in Ireland. Dutch Travel-lers, we were solemnly informed, had evolved from dispos-sessed peasants and individual inadequates over a period of less than a century – despite having, as I later verified with Dr. Okely, their own language, political structure based on kin-ship, typically Traveller economic base, and sharing the strict cleanliness codes observed by Gypsies and Irish Travellers. Even more astonishing was the sight of academics nearly coming to blows over the "alleged" Indian origin of the

Gypsies.

In fact the controversies raging within the teacup of Gypsiology are political controversies masquerading as academic ones. Ironically, the conflicting assertions may all be made in the identical hope that they will influence policymakers. One school of thought maintains that the more distant their origins in time and space, the more "real" we must concede the Travellers to be, and treat them accordingly. The other condemns overemphasis on the exotic, interpreting it as a way of distancing ourselves from the group; this in turn leaves open the possibility of claiming that they are not really "ours" and that we therefore have little or no responsibility towards them. Within weeks of recognising this phenomenon, I saw it come to a head here in Ireland, as the National Council for Travelling People split along precisely these lines.

Underlying all of this discourse is the unspoken assumption that the validity of Gypsy/Traveller culture is up for definition and approval by the majority population. No such debate occurred in the other sections of the minority rights conference. For example, the question of European/Christian responses to the recent influx of Muslim immigrants could be examined from many angles, without anyone feeling a need to address whether Islam is a "real" religion or merely an offshoot of the Judeo-Christian tradition. Islamic validity was taken as given, thus clearing the ground for the next, pragmatic stage: how shall we in Europe deal with our Pakistani, Turkish, Kurdish, Algerian minorities? How shall we establish dialogue? How shall we evolve a compromise between their cultural claims and ours? How shall we ensure that mistrust is not expressed as discrimination? How can we go further, towards a positive, mutually enriching relationship?

From this point of view the origin controversy surrounding Gypsies and Travellers is a smokescreen, a diversion to prevent the addressing of the pragmatic question outlined above. The evolution of Islam, or the history of colonialism and the slave trade, are interesting topics and deserve serious academic consideration, as does the question of the origins of the various Travelling Peoples of Europe. Meanwhile, Muslim, ex-colonial and Traveller minorities require a pragmatic response – hopefully a respectful one – from the majority society. Let us cease to allow uncertainty in the academic field to be used as an excuse for punitive measures in the world at large.

NOTES

[1]   The term "settled" is used here to designate "non-Traveller". It is not a synonym for "sedentary", nor is "Traveller" a synonym for "nomadic". Many Travellers are sedentary, and many settled people move about more than Travellers do.

[2]   A familiar analogy is Black English. Overhearing television, even without visual clues, one can instantly recognise a Black speaker, despite regional variations. Black American English is cohesive and distinctive because of its West African linguistic underlay.

[3]   It is worth noting that Irish Travellers have traditionally lived in houses – from rented cottages to the shantytown shacks to be seen in today's illegal encampments – in the winter months. Living in a house or caravan is not in itself an ethnic indicator. The settled family on caravan holiday do not instantly become Travellers, nor is the Traveller family in a house necessarily showing a desire to assimilate. Housedwelling is an option of accommodation, not identity. This is slowly being recognised by local authorities, who have begun to build "proper" houses in all-Traveller schemes.

[4]   The Italian anthropologist Leonardo Piasere (1985) argues that Gypsies and Travellers are not ignorant illiterates, but have very deliberately rejected literacy, knowing that it would solidify the past, thus imposing a baggage of precedent curtailing flexibility in the present.

[5]   The Irish Traveller Resource Collection – full address in bibliography under Ní Shúinéar – is available for consultation *in situ* or through interlibrary loan. Its unique strength is its eclecticism – it includes *every* reference on Irish Tavellers that comes into its possession, whether from academic/popular/media etc. sources. The compilers urgently request the public at large to contribute to this work by sending in all Traveller-related material (i.e. references in national/provincial press, handbills requesting scrap . . .).

[6]   Leids Universiteits-Fonds (LUF) Centennial Congress, "The Social Construction of Minorities and their Cultural Rights in Western Europe", Leiden, September, 1990.

REFERENCES

Barth, Frederick (ed).   *Ethnic Groups and Boundaries.* London: Allen and Unwin, 1970.

Cash, Anthony   "The Language of the Maguires", *Journal of the Gypsy Lore Society*, 4th Series, Vol. 1, No. 3, 1977.

Commission on Itinerancy   *Report of the Commission on Itinerancy.* Dublin: Stationery Office, 1963

Crawford, M.H.   "Genetic Affinities and Origin of Irish Tinkers", in *Biosocial Interrelations in Population Adaptation.* E.S. Watts, F.E. Johnston and G.W. Lasker (eds.), 93-103. The Hague: Mouton, 1976.

Crawford, M.H. and Gmelch, G.   "The Human Biology of Irish Tinkers: Demography, Ethnohistory and Genetics", *Social Biology* 21, 1974, 321-31.

Gmelch, G.   *The Irish Tinkers: The Urbanization of an Itinerant People,* Menlo Park, California: Cummings Publishing Co., 1977.

Gmelch, G. and Gmelch, S.B.   "The Emergence of an Ethnic Group: The Irish Tinkers", *Anthropological Quarterly*, Vol. 49, No. 4, Oct. 1976 reprinted Dec. 1976. Washington D.C.: The Catholic University America Press, 225-238.

"Ireland's Travelling People: A Comprehensive Bibliography" , *Journal of the Gypsy Lore Society* Vol.3, 1978, 159-169.

Harper, J.   "Gypsy Research in the South", in *The Not so Solid South: Anthropological Studies in Regional Subculture.* K. Kenneth Moreland (ed.), Southern Anthropological Society Proceedings No. 4, UGA Press, 1971.

Kenrick, D.   *How Old Are The Irish Travellers?* Occasional Papers of the Romani Institute No. 2, revised version, 1979.

Macalister, S.

The Secret Languages of Ireland, with special Reference to the Origin and Nature of the Shelta Language. Cambridge: Cambridge University Press, 1937.

Mayall, D.

Defining the Gypsy: Ethnicity, "Race", and Representation. Paper presented to International Conference on Minority Rights, Leiden 1990 (in press).

Ní Shúinéar, S.

On the Ethnicity and Origins of the Irish Travellers, Master's Thesis, Jagiellonian University, Kraków, 1979. Unpublished ms., available from the Irish Travellers Resource Collection, The Library, University of Ulster, Shore Road, Jordanstown, Co Antrim BT37 0QB.

Commentary on Macalister's "The Secret Languages of Ireland", 1979, revised 1984. Unpublished ms., available from the Irish Travellers Resource Collection.

Macalister Debunked: The Case for Critical Assessment of Macalister's Assertions on the Origins of the Shelta Language and of its Speakers, The Irish Travellers, 1984. Unpublished ms., available from the Irish Travellers Resource Collection.

Introduction to the Historical Section of the Irish Traveller Resource Collection, 1985.

The Irish Travellers: "Solving" an Ethnic Minority. Paper presented to International Conference on Minority Rights, Leiden 1990 (in press). Unpublished ms., available from the Irish Travellers Resource Collection.

Okely, J.

The Traveller-Gypsies. Cambridge: Cambridge University Press. 1983.

O'Toole, E.B.

An Analysis of the Life Style of the Travelling People of Ireland. Master's Thesis, N.Y.

University, undated.

Piasere, Leonardo

Connaissance Tsigane et Alphabétisation (Gypsy Knowledge and Literacy), report on Gypsy family education commissioned by the Commission of the European Communities, University of Verona, Psychology Dept. Report No. 26. November 1985, published in part in *School Provision for Gypsy and Traveller Children*, European Community synthesis report, Jean-Pierre Liégeois (ed.), 1986.

ETHNICITY AND IRISH TRAVELLERS: REFLECTIONS ON NÍ SHÚINÉAR

Dympna McLoughlin

INTRODUCTION

Martin Luther King brought Afro-Americans together in the sixties under the twin banners of Black pride and pacificism. Conscious of themselves as a distinct people they demanded the civil rights and liberties denied to them and which other Americans enjoyed. The undisputed fact that Afro-Americans were distinct from Americans of European background provided a strong foundation for group solidarity. The power of this group solidarity, asserted in terms of race, was the basis on which civil rights were subsequently achieved.

This utilisation of the concept of race as the basis of group identity, coupled with a set political and social agenda, is from another context, another people, and another time.[1] In a thirty year timewarp, it now seems fashionable to apply it to Travellers in the Irish context. Not only is the concept inaccurate, it is also detrimental to the cause of Irish Travellers and should be discarded altogether.

In contemporary European terms the concept of race is a very loaded one. The victimisation of people because of their racial origins ushers in images of Holocaust, genocide and its modern-day Balkan version of ethnic cleansing. It connotes fierce and violent obliteration of one group by another. Whilst victimisation and discrimination is also a type of violence, and whilst not wishing to diminish the experiences of Irish Travellers, the same discourses cannot be utilized to describe the position of Travellers in contemporary Ireland,

and the Muslims in civil war torn Bosnia. The situations are not comparable and a different form of discourse is needed.

The claim that Travellers are an ethnic group is one that has aroused considerable controversy (Ní Shúinear, Chap. 4). This debate has been powerful in that it has opened up issues for public discussion that have never been considered before and, as a result, there is communication between Travellers and some sections of the settled community. In this regard the claim to ethnicity has been successful. However, in most other aspects the concept is problematic. On a very general level, can this claim be sustained considering that the National Council for Travelling People is split on the issue? Can half the Travellers of Ireland be considered an ethnic group and the other half not? Ethnicity is an all-embracing term. It cannot be selectively utilised, or reserved for parts of groups.

Ultimately, the claim of some Travellers that they constitute an ethnic group is a most conservative claim. None of the structures, institutions and practices within Irish society which serve to perpetuate inequality, poverty, lack of access and its corollary of social exclusion are addressed in this assertion. Equal participation in the bounty of the state (such as it is) should be available to all Irish citizens and not on a special claims basis.

This paper constitutes a general commentary on Irish Travellers rather than a historical refutation of the concept of ethnicity as applied to a section of that group. Specific problems with the concept of ethnicity will be briefly alluded to, and the main part of the paper will draw on historical material in highlighting the contemporary confusion between Travellers and vagrants.

PART ONE:
THE CLAIM FOR ETHNICITY

In trying to establish this claim of ethnicity a checklist approach has been utilised by Ní Shúinéar in a provocative article in this volume (Ní Shúinear, Chap 4.) The ethnic status of Travellers thus hinges on their racial distinctiveness, a shared set of cultural values, social separation, language, and finally, spontaneous and organised enmity. It is useful to go through some of these.

i)   A Distinct Race

A grave sense of unease is generated when any group makes an assertion to racial distinctiveness. Apart from being very difficult to prove, the historical claims for "pure" races, unblemished by "outside" influences, have supported a eugenics movement this century, as well as tragedy, violence and long-term negative repercussions on a global scale. Biological theories of race are a dangerous starting point in any group's search for identity or solidarity.[2]

ii)   Shared Cultural Values

The common bond in any group of individuals is a sense of shared cultural values. This does not necessarily make them an ethnic group. For example, women may come together, dedicate their lives in poverty, chastity and obedience to God, and spend their days working towards an agreed purpose perhaps as missionaries or educators. In remaining members of such a group, in this instance a religious order, certain values and commitments are shared by all members of the community. This does not make them an ethnic group. Furthermore, shared cultural values are usually negotiated on an ongoing basis between members of the group. Even in the most conservative and defensive of groups they are not totally rigid and immutable. It is therefore not the cultural values *per se* but the consensus of the individuals as to these shared values that determines group membership.

A cultural value which Ní Shúinéar points out is the Travellers' differentiation between public and private space. The private world of home is carefully maintained whilst the public one, the area immediately surrounding the home, is unkept and untidy "as it's somebody else's responsibility" (Ní Shúinear, Chap. 4). This attitude is not unique to the Traveller community. One only has to look at the communal areas of old inner city flat complexes, as well as some of the new large council housing estates, to see the same phenomenon. In these areas, usually of high unemployment, few services, and general deprivation, homes are maintained to a very high standard whilst the public areas, the staircases, yards and any "green areas" that might exist, are neglected. The maintenance of this public space is the responsibility of a public body, and is usually a low priority.

iii) Social Separation

Social separation is the fundamental impulse in the organisation of all societies. The majority of societies known to us have some type of social hierarchy where intermixing amongst the different strata is difficult. In our own society, we realise from a very early age that people with wealth, influence and resources reside in certain parts of our cities and towns, and socialise with each other in clubs and organisations that are exclusive, in that occupations (or more crudely earnings) determine membership. Their offspring will usually attend the same type of schools, and invariably attend university to gain a professional qualification. The poor, by contrast, tend to have little choice where they will live, and many will be placed in council-housing ghettos. "Desirable" residential areas are not found in close proximity to either council housing estates or Travellers' sites. Children of poor families, in both Traveller and settled communities, face all types of obstacles in acquiring both primary and secondary-level education and thus few have a chance to meet and socialise with the wealthy in a university setting. It is argued here that people who are not well-off do not usually meet, socialise, or share educational experiences with the wealthy. Neither do they share equally in the resources of the state. Fairy tales and romantic fiction to the contrary, marriage between classes is rare, and exceptionally so in Ireland. The social separation felt by many Travellers is part of a larger **class** separation. Their feelings of exclusion, marginality and social isolation are replicated within many poor communities.[3]

It is important to make the point that the social separation experienced by Travellers is not self-imposed or seen as desirable by them. It, therefore, cannot constitute an element in establishing a claim for ethnicity. Travellers want to participate fully in Irish society. They want to participate in social and recreational activities as they do in their religious observances. They have the same expressed need to avail of health, welfare and educational facilities as citizens of the state. If they did not want to fully participate in the dominant culture then various charges of discrimination would not arise. Powerful groups deny them access to full participation in society. This separation is imposed upon Travellers and is a cause of concern since it denies them basic civil rights. It is Travellers themselves who are taking cases of discrimination to the Irish Council for Civil Liberties.

iv) Language Barrier

Whilst Travellers have their own language Gammon or Cant, they have no difficulty in communicating with "outsiders" in social, official or trading capacities. The existence of this language is no doubt a very distinctive and important element to their group and individual identity, but again cannot be utilised as a basis to assert a claim of ethnicity. Native Irish speakers may perceive themselves as a most distinctive element in Irish society, as indeed they are, but the vital importance of this living language to this group has nowhere been used to sustain a claim to racial separateness. (Obviously the social and political agenda of the two groups are very different.)

v) Spontaneous and Organised Enmity

In recent years we have witnessed all types of harassment of Travellers from the placing of boulders on their traditional stopping places, to the very public and menacing rage of individuals who will not tolerate Travellers living anywhere in their neighbourhood. Many also will have witnessed the prejudice towards young Traveller children in shops, schools and many other public arenas. There can be no disputing the fact that prejudice and discrimination does exist and is a daily fact of life for Traveller families. Whilst not making light of this prejudice and intolerance it must also be pointed out that not all the venom in Irish society is reserved for the Traveller community.

Religious minorities, also, at certain times felt barely tolerated on this island. This aspect of our history has received but sparse documentation (Ryan 1985; Feely 1982). Similarly, the never-ending intolerance of our society can daily be seen in the treatment of "undesirables", drug addicts, persons recovering from mental illness, the homeless. Because they are powerless, poor, disorganised and inarticulate, the infringements in their human rights and civil liberties rarely merits public comment.[4] Deserted wives and single parents also face social censure; it is only a few years since we rid ourselves of the legal concept of illegitimacy and, still, "bastard" is common parlance for undesirables. Tolerance as a positive attribute, or indeed any attempt to understand difference has never been valued very highly by Irish people, particularly those with the power of a public mandate either in the sacred or secular realm.

PART TWO:
HISTORY AND TRAVELLERS

In this second part of this paper the importance of history is discussed, particularly in relation to those groups excluded from the dominant historical record. A case for the importance of history is made in the establishment of a sense of collective identity amongst all groups. The relevance of history is brought to bear on a misleading confusion (which persists) between the contemporary Traveller and historical vagrant.

Somehow the notion has come about that Travellers are relict survivors of the famine of 1845-47. Having been dispossessed of their land, these people took to the road and have remained as transients into the twentieth century. Whilst, superficially, this may seem like a benign and positive story, in fact it gives a false historical validity to their outcast status. Few Irish individuals owned land before the famine and even fewer immediately afterwards. Thousands of Irish cottiers, labourers and even small farmers were left destitute. Hardship and emigration were experienced by all groups. Post-famine chaos was soon replaced by a new economic order and a political agenda which focussed almost exclusively on land ownership.[5] If we accept the view that Travellers were originally settled, and then part of a dislocated group, the underlying assumption is that this was due to their own personal shortcomings in that they were unable to adapt to a changing world. This inability, according to this logic, remains with them into the twentieth century where they remain on the margins of Irish society.

How do Travellers themselves feel about their origins? Ní Shúinéar points out that Travellers live in a perpetual present and have a very different attitude to their past than the settled community. "They treat the past itself as a sort of baggage, a surfeit of which would tie them down in the present. Instead they cultivate an intense present-time orientation, living in a perpetual now" (Ní Shúinear, Chap. 4).This may mean that Travellers have no interest in written narrative history which is the narrowest interpretation of what history is about. Yet we all carry our history, our memories, around in our heads. Whether we choose to share or write it down is another issue, but the fact remains that all individuals have memories (their histories) just as they have consciousness. They remember not only yesterday, but last month, last year, and occasions of exceptional significance such as a wedding day, the birth of a child, or the death of a parent or spouse.

The absence of marginal groups from the historical records of their own society has become a political issue in the teaching of history. For example, the native people of North America, South Africa, and Australia are totally denied a past in the ethnocentric histories of European discovery and exploration.[6] These previously excluded groups, in establishing themselves in the consciousness of "westerners", have moved first to reclaim their history, and reclaim it in terms that are meaningful and significant to them.

Historians have now commenced to take notice of groups traditionally excluded from teaching and research. Irish women in particular have been articulate in pointing to the great omissions regarding their history and in making a case for those traditionally assumed to be unworthy of research and documentation (Cullen 1985; Luddy and Murphy 1989; McCurtain and O'Dowd 1991; Clear 1991). Histories of the victorious (always male), conquest and war, politics and diplomacy no longer constitute the totality of the historian's endeavours. There has emerged a history of the multiple narrative, encompassing the traditionally excluded and marginalised, a new focus on social, economic and intellectual issues and the innovative utilisation of concepts of representation, power and survival.

While accepting differing views of what constitutes history and how groups themselves may want to utilise it, it is worth pointing out that a search for origins is a good starting point in understanding Travellers and especially in making a claim for separation. That said, a search for origins should not take precedence over immediate and pressing concerns of Travellers as expressed in their own agendas and relating to the quality of their lives in the Ireland of the 1990s.

Very little work has been carried out on Travellers to date. This is not surprising. In his recent book on politics and society in Ireland, J.J. Lee points out that post-independence Ireland did thirst for knowledge but not for knowledge about itself (Lee 1989). Instead of analysing the reality of Irish life (in both academic inquiry and public policy), we participated, he argues, in the public myth of a traditional harmonious Catholic Ireland. The pervasiveness of this myth right up to the present is testimony, Lee asserts, to our heroic capacity for self-deception.

This myth was a response to a particular political climate. The newly-independent state was desperately trying to establish Republicanism on a basis of homogeneity and mass conformity. This sense of Irishness came "naturally" from the dominance of Catholicism and the "shared" experience or rural living which bound all Irish people so neatly together into nationhood. The Irish State was established on this coercive basis and all those individuals and groups who did not fit the bucolic image, so frequently articulated by de Valera, did not belong. If they wanted to stay they had to keep their silence. With censorship of the press, literature and the media, all channels of dissent were effectively denied to them (Carson 1990).

Thus was ushered in the most conservative and stifling period of cultural homogeneity and conformity. All things "foreign" or innovative were despised and the political concept of Irishness was formulated on negativism. "We" were Irish because "we" were against imperialism, secular influences, communism, socialism etc. This coercive sense of nationhood took attention away from internal social conflicts, and the grounds of social, ideological and political debate were effectively narrowed to issues of national self-determination.

A landmark attempt by the Minister of Health, Noel Browne, to legislate for state involvement in the lives of citizens, in the Mother and Child Scheme, was profoundly threatening to the old and newly-established power elites. The issue, because it had the potential to touch the lives of so many citizens, did for a time broaden the parameters of public debate. More significant, perhaps, was the host of conservative and reactionary societies set up to quell debate and "save" the real Ireland. Muintir na Tíre and Macra na Feirme stem from this period as does Opus Dei and their combined concern was to fight off perceived threats to rural Catholic Ireland.

The fact that this place was profoundly repressive for farming women was never relevant. Issues concerning minorities or any type of civil or artistic freedoms had no place on any of these agendas. Fundamental conflicts that existed within rural Ireland between farmers and labourers were gaily glossed over in the promotion of a false image of classless, decent and devotional rural folk.

The numbers of those alienated and excluded by the effects of this dominant myth have only become apparent in recent years. Courageous individuals have looked to the Constitution of the state and to the European Court to claim their personal rights. Significantly, the legal profession and the courts proved to be the most effective avenues for change. Involvement in the European Community has also been important in opening up wider horizons and providing a basis for comparison for beleaguered Irish individuals and groups. They will no longer remain silent and passive. Within the context of a newly independent state, Travellers were viewed as derivative from mainstream Irish culture in the romantic notion of a dispossessed Irish peasantry. There were no arguments for separate ethnic identities, pluralism or the toleration of diversity. In this political climate it was important that Travellers be depicted as both derivative and deviant from mainstream, homogeneous, Irish society. Joining them in their "problem" status were various religious groups of Protestant and Jew, as well as separated individuals, deserted wives, single parents (mostly women), homosexuals and even writers and artists. Ireland from the 1920's up to the 1980's had no room for diversity, pluralism and heterogeneity. Many groups were ignored, censored and made outcast.

PART THREE:
THE ORIGINS OF CONFUSION BETWEEN THE
TRAVELLER AND VAGRANT –
THE NINETEENTH CENTURY BACKGROUND

Nineteenth century Ireland was a very stratified society. It was composed not only of the favourite nationalist dualism of "landlords" and "peasantry" but of various other economic gradations of both men and women in pursuits deemed respectable and otherwise. The poor were also divided broadly into two groups. The first was "deserving" and the latter deemed "undeserving". The poverty of the former group was perceived to be the result of misfortune, illness or accident. That of the latter was due, it was popularly believed, to their own personal defects. They were, therefore, presented as too lazy and feckless to work and support themselves, preferring to be supported by the charity of others. The Government and Poor Law officials, who so easily carried out this classification, acknowledged none of the structures in Irish society responsible for the widespread poverty.[7]

This "undeserving" group may have included Travellers but, for the most part, it was made up of subsistence-based Irish individuals. An important point to note about the "undeserving poor" is that they had their own values and way of life, and, as a result, there was a considerable amount of prejudice and social discrimination against them. They had different definitions of work from the middle classes and were, therefore, viewed as idlers. They also had separate views on the employment of women who were not dependent on the exertions of a husband or partner for her support. Pauper women also had very different child-rearing practices from the prosperous. Their children worked and made an economic contribution to the household economy from a very early age.

These women were penalised for their geographical mobility, for their economic independence, and for not having the appropriate degree of humility and diffidence whilst inmates of workhouses, charitable institutions or when dealing with philanthropists (McLoughlin, in prep.). Yet Travellers were not the same as paupers. The basis of the confusion between both groups may derive from the sharing of various survival strategies, of begging, geographical mobility, and a lack of attachment to the land.

i) Begging

The recent work of feminist historian Mary Cullen documents the widespread practice of seasonal begging by the wives and children of nineteenth century cottiers and labourers. "In the economy of the labouring families begging was women's work. She begged and by begging could support the entire family while it had no other resources" (Cullen 1989). This begging was both seasonal and gender specific. It was most pervasive during the summer months, a time when the man of the household went as a migrant to England or Scotland or indeed parts of Leinster. The combined efforts of both man and woman thus made for the survival of the household economy. These nineteenth century begging women were not identified as either Travellers or Gypsies. In the Poor Law Baronial estimates they are most frequently presented as the wives of labourers. Cottiers and labourers lived for part of the year in comparative independence, but in times of scarcity or crises had to utilise various subsistence survival strategies, the most obvious being begging and spalpeen labour. A further characteristic of these subsistence-based households was their responsiveness to the various economic opportunities that presented themselves in Ireland, Britain, and even North America (Kerr 1942).

ii) Geographical Mobility

Geographical mobility was an essential part of the survival strategy of the poor in the nineteenth century. The extent of this mobility can be gleaned from the reports of the Irish Poor Law commissioners, who despaired at the extent of vagrancy.[8] Men and women, sometimes together, other times alone, travelled the length and breadth of the country seeking work, alms, poor relief or just entertainment at fairs or markets. The workhouses often took in wandering lodgers as they travelled throughout the country. Whilst some few attempts were made by officials to curb this widespread geographical mobility in handing out relief and alms only to inhabitants of a specially curtailed geographical area, for the most part these attempts were unworkable (McLoughlin 1988). The Irish labouring classes were characterised by their mobility and their economic responsiveness. Any openings in the British labour market were quickly filled up by Irish labourers. Both men and women worked as seasonal labourers in England and Scotland.

Yet the poor in the nineteenth century travelled very differently from contemporary Travellers. The whole family did not travel as a unit. Usually the father travelled alone or with his eldest son, both returning home at seasonal intervals. The mobility was only temporary and not lifelong, and, finally, the begging of the wives and children was also seasonal.

In the last decades of the nineteenth century occupational geographical mobility became anathema to "respectable" Irish society. It was a specific type of mobility that was frowned upon. The continuing mobility of the Irish male (leaving his wife and family behind) became acceptable. The mobility of women either alone or accompanied by children was not. Neither was the wholesale movement of families. It is from this period that we might trace the prejudice towards the family mobility of Travellers.

iii) Attachment to the Land

The final stereotype of Irishness is presumed to be a deep attachment to the land. This attachment to the land is another part of the Irish nationalist myth disguising the class nature of nineteenth century Irish society. The obsession was never universal in Irish society but was gender and class based – in particular it was the obsession of the middling-sized male farmer. Cottiers and labourers, when the first opportunities presented themselves, left for the regularity of town employment. Also the emigration destination of Irish individuals is almost entirely urban (Ward 1971; Kennedy 1979; Lees 1979). The majority of the Irish from the 1840's onwards settled in U.S. and Canadian cities and Irishwomen, particularly, had no desire to recreate in North America the conditions they had left behind in Ireland (Diner 1983). They flocked to the large urban industrial centres of the North eastern seaboard of America.

CONCLUSION

Travellers do not figure as a distinctive group amongst the wretched and subsistence-based in nineteenth century Ireland. What can be said with certainty is that Travellers now use similar strategies as nineteenth century subsistence-based groups, albeit in different ways. In view of the fact that these practices are less and less tolerated in this century, the resilience and durability of the Traveller way of life is all the more remarkable.

On a final note, to dispute the claim to ethnicity is not to undermine the sense of group solidarity and individual identities held by travelling people. Travellers do constitute a distinct group within Irish society. They have their own specific concerns and issues, yet at the same time they willingly participate in the broader society. To wish that their process of engagement with the dominant culture should be on their own terms is not an excessive demand. Indeed it is a goal shared by many other groups who strive towards pluralism in Ireland of the 1990s.

NOTES

1   Whilst the concept of race is somewhat passé, it is important to note that the American civil rights campaign was closely watched worldwide. It formed the basis of the civil rights campaign in Northern Ireland as well as sparking academic imaginations into research and teaching on a more democratic and representative world. Civil rights also formed the powerful basis of the women's movement and whilst the discourse of this movement has changed its original impetus has not been forgotten.

2   Feminist critiques of biological arguments have been particularly powerful and as a result there is both major suspicion and deep-rooted cynicism towards any type of biological essentialism. For further clarification of these issues see Birke 1986; Jagger 1983. Biological theories of race have acted as the foundation stone of the eugenics movement. These justified the inferior social status of non-white and non-European groups (note even the negativism of the labels) on the basis of racial inferiority.

3   The marginalisation and exclusion of the long term unemployed and the poor is now acknowledged in Irish society. See the many reports of the Combat Poverty Agency. These include Murphy Lawless 1992; Miller *et al.* 1992. Relevant also is Callan *et al.* 1989, and Daly 1991.

4   This is slowly changing. The National Council for the Status of Women, Simon Community, and the Drug Rehabilitation Institute work and advocate on behalf of these individuals.

5   For a general perusal and very readable account of this period see Hoppen 1984; Lee 1973; Foster 1989.

6   Examples of some of these histories written from the point of view of native people who are totally excluded from traditional European

narrative histories include Brown 1979; Gilbert 1978; Rowley 1970; Middleton 1977.

[7] On the deserving and undeserving poor see Himmelfarb 1985; Burke 1987; Robins 1987.

[8] Report of the Poor Law Commission and various select committee reports and Records of the Poor Law Inquiry 1836.

REFERENCES

Birke, L.	*Women, Feminism and Biology.* Brighton: Wheatsheaf, 1986.
Brown, Dee	*Bury My Heart at Wounded Knee; An Indian History of the American West.* Picador Books, reprint, 1979. First British edition, London: Barrie and Jenkins, 1971.
Burke, H.	*The People and the Poor Law in Nineteenth Century Ireland.* Dublin: Women's Education Bureau, 1987.
Callan, T. *et al*	*Poverty, Income and Welfare in Ireland.* Dublin: ESRI, 1989.
Carson, J.	*Banned In Ireland: Censorship and the Irish Writer.* London: Routledge, 1990.
Clear, C.	*Nuns in Nineteenth Century Ireland.* Dublin: Gill and Macmillan, 1991.
Cullen, Mary	"How Radical was Irish Feminism 1866-1920", in *Radicals, Rebels and Establishments.* P.J. Corish (ed.) Belfast: Appletree Press, 1985.
Cullen, Mary	"Breadwinners and Providers: Women in the Household Economy of Labouring Families, 1835-36" in Luddy and Murphy, 1989, 88-166.
Daly, Mary	*Women and Poverty in Ireland.* Dublin: Attic Press, 1991.

Diner, H.E.   *Erin's Daughters in America.* Baltimore: The
                               Johns Hopkins University Press, 1983.

Feely, Pat   "Aspects of the 1904 Pogrom", *Old Limerick
                               Journal,* Winter 1982, no.11, 18-19.

Foster, Roy   *Modern Ireland 1600-1972.* Penguin Books
                               1989, first published 1988.

Gilbert, Kevin   *Living Black.* Penguin Books, 1978. London:
                               Allen Lane, 1977.

Himmelfarb, G.   *The Idea of Poverty: England in the Early
                               Industrial Age.* New York: Vintage Books,
                               1985.

Hoppen, K.T.   *Elections, Politics and Society In Ireland.*
                               Oxford: Clarendon Press, 1984.

Jagger, A.   "Human Biology in Feminist theory; Sexual
                               Equality Reconsidered", in *Human Biology
                               and Feminist Theory: Sexual Equality Revisited.*
                               C. Gould (ed.). Totowa: Bowman and
                               Allanheld, 1983.

Kennedy, R.E.   *The Irish: Emigration, Marriage and Fertility.*
                               California: University of California Press,
                               1979.

Kerr, B.   "Irish Seasonal Migration to Great Britain
                               1800-1830", *Irish Historical Studies,* 1942, No
                               3, 365-380.

Lee, J.   *The Modernisation of Irish Society 1848-1918.*
                               Gill History of Ireland. Dublin: Gill and
                               Macmillan, 1973.

Lee, J.   *Politics and Society in Ireland 1912-1985.*
                               Cambridge: Cambridge University Press,
                               1989.

Lees, Lynn   *Exiles of Erin: Irish Migrants in Victorian Lon-
                               don.* Manchester: Manchester University
                               Press, 1979.

Luddy, M. & Murphy, C.   *Women Surviving.* Dublin: Poolbeg, 1989.

McCurtain M. & O'Dowd, M.   *Women in Early Modern Ireland.* Dublin: Wolfhound Press, 1991.

McLoughlin, D.   *Women, Sex and Respectability in Nineteenth Century Ireland.* Manuscript in preparation for publication.

McLoughlin, D.   *Shovelling Out Paupers, Female Emigration From Irish Workhouses 1840-1860.* Unpublished Ph.D. thesis. New York: Syracuse University, 1988.

Middleton, Hannah   *But Now We Want The Land Back.* Sydney: New Age Publishers, 1977.

Miller, J., *et al.*   *Lone Parents, Poverty and Public Policy in Ireland.* Dublin: Combat Poverty Agency, 1992.

Murphy Lawless, J.   *The Adequacy of Family Income and Expenditure.* Dublin: Combat Poverty Agency, 1992.

Robins, J.   *The Lost Children: A Study of Charity Children in Ireland.* Dublin: I.P.A. 1980, Reprinted 1987.

Rowley, C.D.   *The Remote Aborigines.* Canberra: Australian National University Press, 1970.

Ryan, Des   "The Jews of Limerick", *Old Limerick Journal,* Winter 1985, no.18, 36-40.

Ward, D.   *Cities and Immigrants: A Geography of Change in Nineteenth Century America.* New York and London: Oxford University Press, 1971.

NOMADISM IN IRISH TRAVELLERS' IDENTITY

Michael McDonagh

Why speak of "nomadism" instead of "travelling" – especially as many Travellers would not use the word, or even understand it? When Travellers speak of travelling, we mean something different from what country people usually understand by it. Many country people, who call themselves "settled", may in fact travel more than some Travellers, but this does not make them nomadic.

Country people travel to get from A to B. But for Travellers, the physical fact of moving is just one aspect of a nomadic mind-set that permeates every aspect of our lives. Nomadism entails a way of looking at the world, a different way of perceiving things, a different attitude to accommodation, to work, and to life in general.

Travellers' views of accommodation differ vastly from those of country people. Travellers see accommodation as a stopping place, whether the stay turns out to be a long one or a short one. Whether living on a halting site or in a house, accommodation is always seen as temporary. The exception would be the family who, as part of the path to assimilation within the settled community, have lost the desire to travel. These families have lost their identity as Travellers and, with it, the feeling inside of longing to be on the move.

A terrifying experience for many Travellers is when they move into a house and begin to face the reality that they are expected by the authorities to remain in this one, permanent, place for the rest of their lives. I remember when I first got a house, my grandfather looked at me and said, "Michael, that's all very well for the winter – but how will you feel when the spring comes in, and you'll see the bumblebee buzzing at your window ... ?" In some cases, Travellers have become physically sick and very depressed when they move into houses, and never adjust psychologically to living in the one place permanently. Many Travellers have left houses for these reasons.

Most Travellers who live in houses are contented enough, as long as we know and feel we can move on when we need to. When we have the option of travelling, we have peace of mind – even though we may not actually exercise that option. But if we get into a situation where we feel we're being forced to settle in a place, that we are being blocked from moving on, it's a different story: the Traveller would not be able to stay with peace of mind, and in most cases would move on.

When I was accommodation officer for the National Council for Travelling People, I talked to Travellers all over the country about this. I wanted to understand these feelings. And one way I had of finding out was, I would ask people, "How would you feel if you were told that you *have* to stay exactly where you are now, for the rest of your life?" And the reaction was just horror.

Just as settled people remain settled people even when they travel, Travellers remain Travellers even when they are not travelling. Travellers who are not moving can, and do, retain the mindset of a nomad. This is why I feel it is important to speak of "nomadism" rather than "travelling" with regard to Travellers.

Nomadism, its functions, and the social ills that accompany forced settlement, all link Irish Travellers with Travellers elsewhere. As the E.C. synthesis report, *School Provision for Gypsy and Traveller Children*, puts it, "A Traveller is someone who remains detached from his surroundings, who is able to pick up and move whenever it is useful or necessary to do so, when he needs to or simply feels like it. There is an important difference between the objective reality of travelling (the fact of moving from one place to another) and the subjective reality: feeling oneself to be a Traveller ... *Nomadism is as much a state of mind as a state of fact.*" (34-35).

THE FUNCTIONS OF NOMADISM

Travellers do not wander aimlessly, with no precise goals to meet. Travellers' nomadism fulfills many functions vital to our very survival. I will discuss these under three broad headings – social, economic, and cultural – while emphasising that there is no such division in real life.

Social

Travellers travel in small groups – a couple of closely related nuclear families – but we understand our family membership in terms of the vast extended family. When we travel, we meet up with other family members, often with a social occasion such as a wedding or funeral involving a family member as the focus of our get-together. Even families who are sedentary for most of the year feel a lot of joy and happiness when setting out on a journey, although it may only be a short one. These feelings are very much in evidence in the way Travellers are participating in the annual Traveller pilgrimage.

Getting together with other members of the family also serves many practical functions, for example, finding suitable marriage partners. Traveller parents arrange their children's matches, preferably within the extended family. Keeping in touch through travel also means keeping tabs on a wide range of potential partners. But keeping tabs on family members applies to everyone. When people meet, they pass on news, including scandal. Travellers live their lives balanced on a thin line, their every move watched by the whole family. If they do anything that brings them close to crossing it, they'll be let know about it in dozens of ways by dozens of people. And if they cross that line, it will be very, very hard to get back on the right side of it.

So, keeping up with news, building contacts, strengthening relationships – these are all strong reasons for travelling: the "pull factors" for nomadism. There are "push factors" too. Just as travelling gives the opportunity of meeting up with people, it also makes it possible to avoid people. This is of *major* importance to Travellers. When arguments arise,

being able to move on means keeping the conflict from
becoming too serious.

But the social reality of nomadism is far greater than the
mere fact of travelling. Country people organise every aspect
of their lives – from neighbourhood watch to parishes to
electoral constituencies – on the fact of sedentarism, the fact
that they live permanently side-by-side with a fixed group of
other people. Travellers, on the other hand, organise every
aspect of their lives around family ties; how far away other
family members may be is of no importance, any more than
how physically close non-family may be. The Traveller's very
identity requires "keeping in touch", and this in turn
requires travel.

Economic

If you ask a country person, "What are you?", the answer
will be, "I'm a farmer", or "a postman", or "a teacher". Country people identify with the work they do – the more specialised, the better. They insist on defining Travellers in this way,
too: we used to be "tinsmiths", now we're "scrap dealers". But
none of this makes any sense from the Traveller point of
view. Ask a Traveller, "What are you?" and the answer will be,
"I'm a McDonagh", or "one of the Joyces", or "Collins".

The essential characteristic of Travellers' economic base is
self-employment. Being your own boss is the important thing
– being free to fit your work into the often unpredictable
demands of the extended family. What you actually work at is
of very little importance: you look for opportunities and
make the best of them. Travelling is part of attending markets and fairs, of doing seasonal work such as potato or fruit
picking. Travellers must travel to earn their living, be it by
scrap collection, hawking, or recycling waste. Travel is essential to our economic survival.

Cultural

Travelling is a fundamental part of Traveller identity. Many
of our values such as the family network and the support
systems it provides are directly related to it.

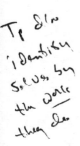

The Irish Traveller Movement, in need of a logo, ran a competition, and it was interesting to see the symbols chosen by entrants. The recurring themes were horses, hoseshoes, wheels, waggons, and tents, even from young Travellers born and reared in houses, who have never been on the road.

Another important symbol of nomadism is jewellery. Like other nomadic peoples all over the world, Irish Travellers carry their wealth by wearing it. I remember, when I was told that I was going to get married, my first thought was, "I'll have to buy her a gold cross and chain". Nobody told me to do it, I just knew that this was what you did. And, over the years, you'd get together other little bits and pieces. Then, when things are at their worst, you always have that to fall back on; it's only ever as a last resort, when you're short of food, short of money, *then* you'd fall back on that piece of jewellery.

insurance savings

like horses

GOVERNMENT POLICY

It would be untrue to say that nomadism is never mentioned in government policy. It is mentioned many times – in fact , it is seen as the entire "problem" to be "solved". Nomadism just got rechristened: "itinerancy".

From 1963 on, there have been many groups, committees and other bodies that have influenced and helped shape government policy. The Commission on Itinerancy, one of the major influences on government policy, issued its Report in 1963.

"All efforts directed at improving the lot of itinerants and at dealing with the problems created by them, and all schemes drawn up for these purposes must always have as their aim the eventual absorption of the itinerants into the general community" (p. 106).

good quote

I feel that this quotation, taken from the Report and expressing in a few words what the Report says over and over again in different ways, was the start of a long drawn out campaign to get rid of Travellers' nomadism, blaming the Travellers as

same in UK

the creators of the problem and saying that all schemes should take them away from their nomadic way of life and absorb them into the general community. Thus, "the itinerant problem" was born.

The Commission went on to say,

"Insofar as the itinerants are concerned, absorption into the general community can be achieved only by a policy of inducing them to leave the road and to settle down" (p. 106).

The Commission went on to make many recommendations on how to deal with "the itinerant problem". The methods used to induce Travellers to settle down were, and are, severe:

"It should be made an offence with adequate penalties, (including imprisonment), for itinerants to camp within a stipulated radius of an approved camping site provided by a local authority . . . The minimum penalties for disregarding (this rule) should be considerably more than the camping fees for a week on the approved camping site" (p. 56).

"The Commission consider it essential that any special difficulties and obstacles in the way of itinerant families obtaining any of the State or local authority allowances for which they are eligible should be eliminated as far as possible as a means of inducing them to settle . . ." (p. 75).

"The procedure which requires unemployment applicants to register at regular intervals is one that it is felt could be used to encourage qualified itinerants to settle in one locality provided, of course, that they were so allowed. The Commission can see no objection in these circumstances to a provision which would require a person of no fixed abode to register at more frequent intervals than the regulation requires for the settled population" (p. 76).

" . . . a substantial amount of the state and local authority assistance including children's allowances given to those itinerants who have not settled down in a fixed abode or who are not regularly

spending lengthy periods on an approved camping site provided for them . . . should be paid in voucher form exchangeable for food and clothing so as to overcome abuse by dissipation on intoxicating liquor . . . Those who settle down should, after a probationary period . . . be paid and treated in every way the same as members of the settled population" (p. 76-77).

"In cases of conviction of persons of no fixed abode, any fines imposed should be payable forthwith" (p. 100).

"It will be vitally necessary for the success of any scheme for the absorption and rehabilitation of itinerants to have in each area where it is proposed to settle a number of itinerant families, local voluntary committees, . . . who are prepared to interest themselves directly in the settlement of the families concerned . . . to obtain their confidence and then to encourage them to learn and adopt the ways of settled life . . ." (p. 106).

Following the publication of the Report, such voluntary bodies, known as Itinerant Settlement Committees, were set up all over the country. The job of many of these Committees was, and in some cases still is, to "settle" Travellers and get them assimilated into the settled community.

Eleven years later, in 1974, a book called *Travelling People* was published. This was a collection of essays on various aspects of the Travellers. Although it was not an official government publication, the contributors were all prominent advisors to the government, so this gives us an idea of how their thinking had changed in that period.

I feel that, for a book that came out not so long after the Report, people here were expressing very progressive ideas; for example the word "Traveller" is used, instead of "itinerant", and is always capitalised. There is also the recognition that Travellers are *not* all the same, and that you cannot define the needs of one and then generalise this for all. There is even recognition that they shouldn't be discouraged by mistakes in "settlement", but they should learn from them (Sholdice 1974, 119). The reason for this, though, is that

" . . . if the family does not like the accommodation it is given, it will leave and go back on the road. That particular attempt at settlement will have been a failure, and we will all be 'back to square one' " (Sholdice 1974, 121).

So, not making it in a house is seen as a failure, and moving from a house is seen as a step backwards. Yet to this day, many Travellers that are the most nomadic are also the most economically successful, and also have far less difficulty with their identity than people forced into settlement. Country people are not able to see this; for them, just being mobile is negative and wrong in itself.

The National Coordinator for Itinerant Settlement, Joyce Sholdice, wrote of nomadic Travellers:

"Whatever their reasons are, the decision to remain mobile is theirs and must be respected, provided they do not infringe on the rights of other people" (Sholdice 1974, 131).

This looks very positive, but underneath it all lies the conviction that nomadism is not a valid way of life, and the move to continuously settle and assimilate Travellers remains the goal:

"If no legal, authorised halts are provided, they will continue to park in unsuitable places and cause annoyance to the settled population as well as hardship to themselves. To add to that, their continued presence on the road will mitigate against the settlement and integration of others" (Sholdice 1974, 132).

At the end of the day nomadic Travellers are setting a bad example.

It was not until twenty years after the original Report that a second official government policy statement, this time from the Travelling People Review Body, was issued. Many of the recommendations and statements in this report seem at first to be very progressive and forward thinking; this unfortunately is not at all true. Consider, for example, the following statement, listed as a basic objective:

"To provide within a relatively short number of years a house for all Traveller families who desire to be housed. Travellers who are not so accommodated cannot hope to receive an adequate education. Nor can they avail satisfactorily of services such as health and welfare which are of such significance in the life of all people" (p. 15).

Here we see a recommendation that families who desire a house should be provided with one but, if they don't want a house, they cannot avail satisfactorily of services; no provision is made for meeting the educational needs of nomadic children, nor of providing services to accommodate nomadic families.

Following Joyce Sholdice's 1974 classification, the Review Body states:

"It is unwise to generalise and assume to know what are the requirements of all Travellers, but an outline of different categories of Traveller was adopted for the purposes of this review. On the basis of aspirations, four broad groupings are listed :

a) Families who wish to live in a standard house among settled people.

b) Families who wish to live in a house but situated among their own people, i.e. group housing.

c) Families who wish to remain living in a caravan in a place on which they are entitled to park, with the benefit of amenities.

d) Families who wish to continue travelling but who would avail of authorised serviced sites on which they can remain as long as they wish" (p. 33).

This recognition of difference looks very positive, but, again, the real thinking emerges a few pages later:

"Newly-wed couples who have to occupy caravans following their marriage should be considered extra sympathetically for housing to lessen the risks of regression to a travelling way of life and consequential negativing of the benefits of permanent accommodation and education" (p. 45).

Here we see clearly that "the travelling way of life", that is, nomadism, is considered to be a "regression" from sedentarism. The negative view of nomadic lifestyle has not changed.

On the face of it, there is a very big difference between "solving the itinerant problem" and recognising that "the decision to remain mobile is theirs and must be respected." This change can be illustrated very dramatically with two quotations from the same, extraordinarily influential, politician Charles J. Haughey. As Parliamentary Secretary to the Minister for Justice, he addressed the inaugural meeting of the Commission on Itinerancy in July 1960 :

"there can be no final solution of the problems created by itinerants until they are absorbed into the general community" (Commission on Itinerancy, p. 111).

Thirty-one years later, addressing the Fianna Fáil Árd-Fheis as Taoiseach, he had a very different message:

"Local Authorities throughout the country will be called upon to take special urgent action in this anniversary year to meet the needs of all Travellers within their area and we should respect the culture of our Travelling community and develop a better public understanding of their time honoured way of life" (Presidential Address, 1991).

The rhetoric has certainly changed but has practice?

THE REAL WORLD

Accommodation

"The design prevents access to the back of the houses, leaving only enough space to be able to walk around to the rear. Design is substandard; in some cases they resemble the old tigeens". This was my description, in 1983, of new local authority housing for Travellers, when I was asked to look into this as part of my work as accommodation officer for the National Council.

Some people may say that such bad design is done out of ignorance of our lifestyle. I would say, no. Not out of ignorance. Quite the opposite. Those in power are well aware of the needs of Travellers, and design accommodation to prevent us from maintaining our culture, our work patterns, our social ties.

Another aspect of accommodation, apart from the design, is location. Sites are to be found next to tipheads and cemeteries, and up the sides of mountains in the middle of nowhere. No one, Traveller or settled, would choose to live in such places, and many Travellers refuse to. More than one site has lain idle since the day it was opened.

Boulders

To travel in Ireland today is becoming more and more difficult, if not impossible. One has only to look at the roadside to see the huge boulders blocking the places where Travellers could have stopped. Mounds of clay and rubble, and deep trenches, all serve the same purpose.

The blocking up of the traditional camping places all around the country has been a systematic move to leave Travellers with no place to go. In future, when we look at these boulders, will we see them as monuments to prejudice?

One of the effects of this policy is that when Travellers move into an area, they are afraid to move out, because the camp will be blocked up and they will be unable to return. So, for many Travellers, the only time they feel free to travel is when they have acquired a more permanent place to come back to. I remember one woman who was years camping in the same place, and who fought long and hard for a group housing scheme to be built there. When it was finished, she said to me, "Now I have a house, I can travel at last!" Now, that might seem strange, but I knew what she meant. She couldn't move from that spot, until she had a guarantee she could come back to it.

Prohibition Orders

Prohibition Orders come under the Local Government (Sanitary Services) Act 1948. This is how they work: the local authorities provide accommodation, which may or may not be suitable, for a number of Traveller families. The number seems to be picked out of a hat – it is never the actual number of families in the area, or even a certain percentage of these families. Once the accommodation exists, prohibition orders barring all Travellers from every other part of the area come into effect. Prohibition orders criminalise Travellers for the very fact of being Travellers. Over the past few years they have become a more and more common means of harassing Travellers, and forcing them to move on. The Constitution gives central importance to the family within Irish society. The effect of prohibition is very often to break up families.

Adaptation

As we have seen, the current situation is one in which a range of powerful forces work together to limit nomadism.

Many Travellers have successfully adapted to these limitations. They survive economically, socially, and culturally, with a strong and positive sense of their Traveller identity. The most outstanding success story are the famous Rathkeale-based families, with their Dallas-style mansions. These are only a winter base. In fact these families are highly nomadic for much of the year, travelling throughout the British Isles and lately also the United States. That they are doing very well economically is clear to anybody; what surprised me about them was their better-than-average knowledge of Gammon. Yet on second thought, this is not so surprising: Gammon is a living language for them, because they are so active in trading.

The Rathkeale Travellers upset the apple cart for settled policymakers, who define the Travelling way of life as not being able to fit in with the modern world, and so these living contradictions are not recognised as being Travellers at all. When I talked with them, and told them that as far as policymakers are concerned, they are "traders", not

Travellers, they said, "Well, Michael, you've met us, and you've talked with us. And we would ask you now, that any time you hear that kind of talk, to stand up and tell the truth: that we are Travellers, and proud to be Travellers."

At the other end of the scale, though, are those who have been unable to cope. The policy of forcing Travellers to stay put, and that in large, mixed groups, has eaten into Travellers social structure, economic base, and cultural identity. We have already seen how all of these are bound up with nomadism – they cannot function without it. For example, as members of the extended family lose touch, parents have a smaller number of suitable potential marriage partners for their children. Family support systems break down. People step out of line with no one to put them back on the right track. To quote a Council of Europe document, "Gypsies and Travellers" (1987),

> "When travel becomes just a dream, a long-delayed dream for the Traveller, despair and its effects set in (illness, breakup of the family, aggressiveness and delinquency). The result is a crisis in the society . . ." (Liégeois 1987, 54).

And it's not a simple one-way thing, of having nomadism taken away. The policymakers who do that, also make sure that Travellers are getting a great deal of "help" to "integrate" into "the community". The system makes people dependent on it, taking pride and independence away with one hand and giving the dole and second-hand clothes with the other. It makes no secret of its mission to "help the poor unfortunates", to "rehabilitate" Travellers; and Travellers, seeing how they are regarded, may internalise this low, negative self-image. Once they have accepted that being a Traveller is something to be ashamed of, the next step is to try to change, to become a settled person. And once you do that, you're lost. Because the settled people won't have you, and the Travellers won't want you any more than you want them. And where are you, without your identity? Many Travellers find themselves stuck in limbo, with parents ashamed of their relatives and children ashamed of their parents.

CONCLUSIONS

At the end of the day, the problems faced by Travellers today can be traced back to the interference of settled people who, with their "settlement" committees, have done all they could to *solve the itinerant problem* by putting a stop to *itinerancy*, to nomadism. From 1963 onwards, settled people were certain what they wanted to do, and how to go about doing it. At present, however, they are no longer so sure. This is for two reasons: first, the old ideas haven't worked; second, Travellers themselves are standing up and saying so.

Now is a time of transition, of uncertainty, and I feel that this is a very hopeful sign. There are new moves towards policies based on partnership with Travellers, and on recognition of Traveller ethnicity. Here at home, there is the Irish Traveller Movement, a national movement of both Travellers and settled people who support our claims. Irish people generally are more outward-looking now, with more contact with, and more openness to, new ideas. As settled people get more used to listening to ideas from Italy and Belgium, they may be more willing to listen to ideas from Travellers at home. Travellers, too, are opening up: the Irish Traveller Movement has links with Gypsy and Traveller organisations all over Europe, and there is Irish Traveller representation on the World Romani Congress.

"When we talk about the Travelling community it's not just a question of whether they want housing or whether they would prefer serviced halting sites. It's that they want their culture recognised, they want to be full citizens of this country. I think that the most important things are that there's real space for their own self-development and self-expression, that we have space for them and that we value them; and that the other things like the appropriate kind of houses, services and facilities are provided to the best of our ability as a nation. But perhaps the most important thing is that we value them as a distinct community within our larger community."

(extract from a speech given by President Robinson at a conference organised by the Irish Association and Dublin

Travellers' Education and Development Group on 1st December 1990 at which she suggested the idea of an awards scheme for the design of Travellers' accommodation.)

President Robinson's words express the new spirit of pluralism, the use of imagination to move out of narrow-minded thinking and to move forward in a more accepting manner, in a partnership, in an understanding that differences can be complementary rather than destructive to one another.

REFERENCES

Commission of the European Community — *School Provision for Gypsy and Traveller Children: a Synthesis Report.* Luxembourg, 1987.

Commission on Itinerancy — *Report of the Commission on Itinerancy.* Dublin: Stationery Office, 1963.

Liégeois, Jean-Pierre — *Gypsies and Travellers.* Strasbourg: Council of Europe, 1987.

Sholdice, Joyce — "The Settlement of Travelling People" in *Travelling People,* Victor Bewley (ed.). Dublin: Veritas Publications, 1974, 117-34.

Travelling People Review Body — *Report of the Travelling People Review Body.* Dublin: Stationery Office, 1983.

ETHNICITY AND IRISH TRAVELLERS

John O'Connell

"Being a Traveller follows from the generations, its in our backgrounds. I'm proud I'm a Traveller – you feel free. If a person says to me 'what are you?' I'll say Traveller."

Kathleen McDonagh,
Dublin-based Traveller

"Being a Traveller is the feeling of belonging to a group of people. Knowing through thick or thin they are there for you, having the support of family systems, having an identity."

Michael McDonagh,
Navan-based Traveller

In our ordinary daily lives and in our social transactions we frequently describe who we are individually in terms of a shared collective identity. We call ourselves male or female, Irish, English, French or whatever. As well as identifying with a specific gender and nationality we may on occasion identify with a particular religion, political ideology, skin colour or language group.

In Ireland, we are accustomed to answering questions related to some of these categories in census forms or in making applications for driving licences, passports, marriage and birth certificates. We are less accustomed to answering questions related to ethnicity. In the United States the 1970 Census asked specifically about "colour or race". The Australian Census also asked about "racial origin". In the U.K. the Census did not ask any direct questions relating to ethnicity until 1991. There were, however, indirect questions concerned with ethnic origin in the earlier censuses which asked about place of birth of parents. In 1978 a White Paper on the 1981 Census announced that "a direct question on ethnic origin" was being considered. This gave rise to considerable debate and a postponement until the 1991 Census.

The debates about Irish ethnicity have been largely confined to Britain where Irish people are faced with the issue of declaring or not declaring their ethnicity. This in itself is revealing. Ethnicity is a term we Irish may sometimes use to describe others but not ourselves. It is associated with the strange and exotic and may even have negative connotations attached to it. Yet we have less difficulty in accepting the term when applied to the Irish in the United States. When the word has been used in recent years to describe Travellers it has met with strong resistance and rebuttal. Even when some people admit that they do not know what ethnicity means they insist that whatever it means it does not apply to Travellers! It is important therefore to examine how the term ethnicity is used and how it is understood in social theory and to explore the relevance of this for Travellers.

In sociology and anthropology ethnicity is seen as a cultural and social phenomenon. It is understood: "as a symbolic meaning system, a way for a 'people' to organise social reality in terms of their cultural similarities and differences" (Tovey 1989, 8). Ethnicity, then, "defines the salient features of a group that regards itself as in some sense (usually, many senses) distinct" (Cashmore 1984, 98).

These salient features which distinguish one group from another are sociocultural, such as: a shared feeling of common identity, a sense of a long shared history, of a common descent and place of origin, a common lifestyle, a shared set of values, customs, traditions, language, religion and morality. While ethnicity is not a racial phenomenon nor a biological given, ethnic groups tend to be biologically self-reproducing. The salient features are transmitted from one generation to the next and children are reared to accept these as normal. This gives the impression that ethnicity is a 'natural' and immutable entity. In reality, however, ethnicity is something which is produced in historically specific contexts and it emerges, changes and adapts in meaning over time.

Ronald Cohen in his analysis of ethnicity makes the following statement: "The view of ethnicity accepted here is one in which the identities of members and categorisations by others is more or less fluid, more or less multiple, forming nesting hierarchies of we/they dichotomizations" (Cohen 1978, 359).

Since ethnicity refers primarily to the set of socio-cultural traits which define a shared identity, this raises the question of membership and nonmembership. It is through the process of interaction with other cultural groups, whereby certain features are interpreted as giving a group its identity, that ethnicity is constructed. An awareness of a collective identity and of membership of an ethnic group becomes possible in the context of diverse cultural groups. Isajiw defines an ethnic group as "an involuntary group of people who share the same culture, or descendants of such people who identify themselves and/or are identified by others as belonging to the same involuntary group" (Isajiw 1974, 122).

According to this definition membership of an ethnic group is primarily something which exists independently of individual will or choice, although identification with the group may be optional. While acknowledging that there is a subjective dimension in recognising one's distinctive identity as different from that of others, as well as an objective process whereby others select traits which form the basis of differentiation, ethnicity is not just a matter of personal choice.

"The young people will be ashamed of being a Traveller in the future, however, no matter what you put on them – if it was silk you'd still know them. Its hard to burn wildness out a wild bird's nose – you'll tame them for a while but they'll fly away again."

Paddy McDonnell,
Dublin-based Traveller

"Yet the ethnic affiliation cannot be freely dropped as if a cultural option; frequently, it is deeply embedded in the consciousness through years of socialization within the ethnic group. The ethnic boundary is difficult to break out of" (Cashmore 1984, 99).

Some people may find this too nebulous and demand an answer to the question "does so-and-so belong to an ethnic group?", but as Cashmore states: "The whole point about ethnicity is that it is as real as people want it to be" (Cashmore 1984, 100).

Members and non-members of an ethnic group may not always agree on membership criteria. The sociocultural features which are associated with a particular ethnic group are not innate or fixed, they are selected and given meaning through interaction between groups. Over time, some of these features take on new meaning as they become associated with the group's historical roots. They come to symbolise the group's sense of peoplehood and aspirations, like, for example, nomadism for Travellers.

As referred to earlier, an ethnic group will have a boundary which marks it off from other ethnic groups:

"By emphasising the features of life, past and present, they share, they define boundaries inside which they can develop their own particular customs, beliefs and institutions – in short, their own cultures" (Cashmore 1984, 98).

Such a boundary is established when an ethnic group is recognised as possessing certain physical or cultural characteristics that enable outsiders to identify its members. In order for a group to retain its ethnic identity, it must maintain this boundary between itself and other groups:

"Ethnic group formation is a continuing and often innovative cultural process of boundary maintenance and reconstruction" (Cohen 1978, 397).

This involves many different dimensions:

"Ethnic group affiliations and identifications are complex social, political, and psychological processes in modernised societies" (Banks 1988, 57).

One of the main implications of all this is that the quantity and quality of communication and interaction among group members has to differ from that which takes place with non-members. Ethnic group members will experience a solidarity between one another which extends beyond family relations and neighbours. On the other hand cross-group interaction will be more restricted and will tend to be confined to limited roles and relations which are largely instrumental.

Since ethnicity has to do with a mechanism for differentiating groups from one another it presupposes diverse cultures and socio-economic contexts. In other words we only become conscious of our ethnicity in the context of inter-ethnic relations. Perhaps it is not surprising, therefore, that in Ireland there is a low level of awareness of ethnicity as a phenomenon within Ireland. Irish society has been characterised as being fairly homogeneous – most people are white, the English language is widespread, Roman Catholicism is the dominant religion. As Professor Liam Ryan comments:

"All this reflects one dimension of the Irish experience at least of the Republic of Ireland: that we are basically a well-integrated, cohesive society with no great divisions of creed, class, colour or race; that for the past fifty years we have had a unified society with well-defined and moderate aspirations, where change has not been a disruptive force; that all the major and influential social groupings in Ireland – employers, farmers, shopkeepers, the professions, trade unions, civil service, the churches, political parties – all exhibit a traditional conservative mentality, that Ireland is at heart a contented society, balanced and self-contained, at ease with itself and with the rest of the world" (Ryan 1984, 97-98).

Of course Ryan acknowledges that this is a one-dimensional view of Irish society. It may be the view of a large number of people who do well out of the system and are at ease with the way society is. However, there is an alternative view which a growing number of people see as being more realistic. It is a view which sees Ireland divided on the basis of wealth and poverty, power and powerlessness. As Ryan describes it:

"Ireland's development has been too fragmented politically and culturally, and too impoverished economically to enable us to present with any credibility an image of equanimity to the world" (Ryan 1984, 98).

A closer look at Irish society, therefore, reveals major divisions in terms of class, gender, power, wealth, education, beliefs and values. Another source of social cleavage, frequently overlooked, is in relation to cultural differences. The widespread assumption of monoculturalism is reflected in the education system and in the lack of political will to introduce anti-racist legislation, for instance. It is also evident in the persistent refusal to acknowledge the separate cultural identity of Travellers.

Travellers are one of the largest minority groups in Ireland who see themselves and are seen by others as a distinct group based on their values, beliefs, customs and nomadic way of life. Despite the efforts in recent years of many Travellers and Traveller support groups to achieve recognition as an ethnic group there is a great reluctance among "settled" or sedentary people in general and by the state to grant such recognition. This raises the issue of power, domination and subordination and the relationship of these to the emergence of ethnic identity.

The understanding of this issue presented by Tovey et al. is worth quoting:

"Dominant ethnicity contrasts sharply with subordinate ethnicity. The one enjoys both political and economic power, as well as cultural presumption, while the other, in extreme cases, may be so marginal as to be at the centre of nothing in the larger system but its own ethnic world".

And, again, the members of the dominant group can maintain their position even unconsciously:

"Because of their history of economic sufficiency and the presumed universal validity of their way of life, they tend to claim for themselves the mantle of universalism, to be models to which all others can aspire

and be assimilated into: they purport to be beyond ethnicity" (Tovey 1989, 8).

"Settled" people are the dominant group as far as Travellers are concerned. All key social institutions are controlled by sedentary people – government, police, civil service, education, churches, media and the economy. For most sedentary people nomadism is an aberration because it deviates from the norm i.e. sedentarism. Consequently, when sedentary people make interventions "to help" Travellers there is a strong likelihood that such interventions may be ethnocentric.

Government policy in relation to Travellers has been strongly influenced by an assimilationist ideology. This has, until recently, been supported wholeheartedly by the voluntary sector. The evidence for this can be found, on the one hand, in the government settlement and rehabilitation programme combined with increased restrictions on travelling. On the other hand, it can be seen in the work of itinerant settlement committees which played an important role in the implementation of the recommendations of the government Commission on Itinerancy.

Sedentary people frequently find an explanation for the distinctiveness of Travellers solely in terms of poverty and deprivation. If a "different way of life" is acknowledged at all it is usually seen as a "sub-culture of poverty" which would disappear if the problems of poverty were solved. When in reality it is found that not all Travellers are poor one would expect that the sub-culture of poverty theory would be rejected. Not so. Instead wealthy Travellers are excluded from the theoretical framework by refusing to accept them as "real Travellers" and by defining them as "traders". A typical example of this was reported in the newspapers recently when a group of well-off Travellers were charged in court with trespassing by Dublin County Council. A spokesperson for the Council told the judge

"that the people concerned were not travellers in the sense that they required accommodation from the council. They were in the antique

business, were very well off, and had registered addresses in Rathkeale, Co. Limerick, and in Co. Cork" (Irish Times, 3.9.91).

In reality however, many relatively wealthy Travellers do retain their distinctive identity and because of their economic independence are in a better position than their poorer cousins to retain a nomadic way of life. They may own their own houses and be self-employed. Therefore they are not dependent on the state for accommodation or social welfare. They can purchase good quality trailers and vehicles to tow them with. Nonetheless, despite their relative wealth, these Travellers also experience discrimination and social ostracism, although it may not be on the same scale as that experienced by the majority of Travellers. As the Economic and Social Research Institute report on Travellers pointed out, all Travellers, in contrast to sedentary people, are in some way subordinate in Irish society because they

"are a minority usually without ready access to the power and authority structures within the society in general" (Rottman 1986, 63).

Because of their subordinate position vis-a-vis the dominant population i.e. sedentary people, Travellers are expected to conform to the expectations of the dominant group. They are expected to behave in a "normal way", to live in a house, to abandon a nomadic way of life and to share the same aspirations as the dominant sector. Some Travellers may try to deny or hide their identity in the hope of gaining social acceptance. Others who wish to retain their distinctive identity fear that any further labels such as ethnicity may result in even greater discrimination because being "different" may be interpreted as being inferior. The problem with this strategy of seeking invisibility, apart from the fact that it often does not work, is that it usually reflects not having a healthy sense of ethnic identity, and this can have negative psychological consequences.

Despite the pressures to assimilate and to become invisible, most Travellers, rich and poor alike, manifest an amazing resilience and ability to retain a common identity. Wealth doesn't automatically bring absorption into the mainstream middle classes, for instance. Neither does poverty mean that Travellers will become unidentifiable from marginal working class groups who also experience poverty and deprivation. Likewise in different contexts – urban and rural Ireland, Britain and the United States – Travellers have shown that they can resist assimilation and maintain a boundary between themselves and others.

In exploring the issue of Traveller identity it is important to recognise that consciousness of ethnicity tends to grow in situations of oppression and poverty. As Cashmore states: "Material deprivation is the most fertile condition for the growth of ethnicity" (Cashmore 1984, 102).

In recent years, as Travellers grow in their understanding of the root causes of their social exclusion, there has also been a strengthening in their awareness of their ethnicity. This is partly a defensive mechanism in the face of widespread prejudice, antagonism and discrimination. It is also a political instrument for the achievement of basic human rights. The relevance of this becomes clear when one considers ways to protect Travellers against discrimination. In other words, the significance of a fully legitimated ethnic identity becomes evident when Travellers look for legislation which will guarantee their rights.

Since Ireland does not have anti-racist legislation and has not ratified the U.N. Convention on the Elimination of All Forms of Racial Discrimination it is worth turning to the 1976 Race Relations Act in Britain. Section 3 of the Act states that discrimination may take place on "racial grounds", and "racial groups" is taken to mean "persons defined by reference to colour race, nationality or ethnic or national origins" (Forrester 1985, 96).

Subsequently, the term "ethnic" in the 1976 Act was defined by the House of Lords in the following manner:

"The term 'ethnic' in section 3 of the 1976 Act was to be construed relatively widely in a broad cultural and historic sense. For a group to constitute an 'ethnic group' for purposes of the 1976 Act it had to

regard itself, and be regarded by others, as a distinct community by virtue of certain characteristics, two of which were essential. First it had to have a long shared history, of which the group was conscious of distinguishing it from other groups, and the memory of which is kept alive, and second it had to have a cultural tradition of its own, including family and social customs and manners, often but not necessarily associated with religious observance. In addition, the following characteristics could also be relevant, namely (a) either a common geographical origin or descent from a small number of common ancestors, (b) a common language, which did not necessarily have to be peculiar to the group, (c) a common literature peculiar to the group, (d) a common religion, (e) the characteristic of being a minority or being an oppressed or a dominant group within a larger community" (Forrester 1985, 96-97).

While Gypsies were seen as fitting this definition it was not certain that other Travellers would be given such recognition. The Commission for Racial Equality stated its views in a report in 1980:

"We take the view that Gypsies in the U.K., who number about 50,000 constitute an ethnic minority group and as such are protected against discrimination under the Race Relations Act 1976" (Forrester 1985, 100).

In order to ensure the inclusion of Irish Travellers in the legal interpretation of the 1976 Act a test case would have to be taken.

In Ireland the Prohibition of Incitement to Hatred Bill 1989 made an important step towards the recognition of Travellers' ethnicity by naming Travellers as a distinct group in the Bill. The growing public awareness of the fact that Travellers experience widespread social exclusion is likely to create the conditions necessary for the explicit mention of Travellers in future legislation. Certainly groups working for Travellers' rights who accept what Cohen says in an article on ethnicity, that "individuals are also fated to obtain more or less rewards because of their group identities and categorisation" (Cohen 1978, 402) and that "many inequalities remain group determined", will need to campaign for a system of justice that includes not only individual but group rights as well. Only in this way will the efforts to promote the cultural rights and identity of Travellers be successful.

REFERENCES

Banks, James A.   *Multiethnic Education: Theory and Practice.* Boston: Allyn and Bacon, Inc., 1988.

Barth, Fredrik (ed.)   *Ethnic Groups and Boundaries.* London: Allen and Unwin, 1969.

Cashmore, Ernest   *Dictionary of Race and Ethnic Relations.* London: Routledge and Kegan Paul, 1984.

Cohen, Ronald   "Ethnicity: Problem and Focus in Anthropology", *Annual Review of Anthropology* 7, 1978, 379-403.

Fogarty, Michael P.,   *Irish Values and Attitudes: The Irish Report of*
Liam, Ryan, Joseph Lee   *the European Value Systems Study.* Dublin: Dominican Publications, 1984.

Forrester, Bill   *The Travellers' Handbook: a Guide to the Law affecting Gypsies.* London: Interchange Books, 1985.

Geertz, Clifford   *The Interpretation of Cultures.* New York: Basic Books, 1973.

Greeley, Andrew M.   *Why Can't They be Like Us? America's White Ethnic Groups.* New York: Dutton, 1975.

Isajiw, W.W.   "Definitions of Ethnicity", *Ethnicity* 1, 1974, 111-24.

Rottman, David B.   *The Population Structure and Living Circum-*
Dale Trussing,   *stances of Irish Travellers,* ESRI Paper No.
Miriam M. Wiley   131. Dublin: Economic and Social Research Institute, 1986.

Tovey, Hilary,   *Why Irish? Language and Identity in Ireland*
Damian Hannan,   *Today.* Dublin: Bord na Gaeilge, 1989.
Hal Abramson

THE SUB-CULTURE OF POVERTY RECONSIDERED

Patricia McCarthy

This paper is a refutation of the sub-culture of poverty theory as it relates to Travellers. As the researcher responsible for the original work applying this theory to Irish Travellers, it has been my intention for a long time to publicly refute it, but pressure of other commitments meant that it has not been done until now. Therefore, I welcome the opportunity this volume offers to finally state my position on the issue publicly.

It is nearly twenty years since the original study was done in Galway. The data for this study were collected by means of participant observation in a Traveller's site. This was an innovative research method in sociology at the time and remains so. The data are still valid today and the study is one of the few of Irish Travellers that was based on first hand knowledge. The work of the Gmelchs a few years later and that of Sinéad Ní Shúinéar greatly expanded the base of knowledge about Irish Travellers.

My own study was confined to a group of families in Galway, who were living by the roadside and as such was limited in its applicability. However, the major problem with the study was its theoretical framework. Titled *Itinerancy and Poverty – a Study in the Sub-Culture of Poverty*, it was very much a product of thinking and concepts in sociology at the time. The concept of a culture or sub-culture of poverty was fashionable. This theory, prepared by Oscar Lewis, an American anthropologist, sought to make sense of the phenomenon of inter-generational poverty.

THE SUB-CULTURE OF POVERTY
AND IRISH TRAVELLERS

Lewis listed a large number of traits which were supposedly peculiar to the poor, specifically the long-term poor, people whose parents and grandparents had also been poor. These traits included such characteristics as: present-time orientation, inability to defer gratification, poor self-image, loss of self-respect, large numbers of single parents, families headed by women and so on. The theory was that poverty was cultural and inherited. Certain behaviour patterns were seen to be passed on from one generation of poor people to the next, their behaviour patterns ensuring that they stayed poor. Most of the data collected to corroborate this theory was collected in Latin America.

Several very widely-published books such as *La Vida* were written by Lewis containing studies of poverty done by him using this theoretical framework. It led to specific policy options in relation to the elimination of poverty. The emphasis was put on education and training to break the cycle of poverty. Attention was diverted away from the structural causes of poverty – the economic class system and the in-built institutionalised barriers to social mobility within social systems of capitalist society.

These major flaws with the sub-culture of poverty theory were to be quickly pointed out by other leading social theorists such as Valentine (1968) and the theory was largely discredited within a matter of years.

The sub-culture of poverty theory is not a particularly relevant concept today, even though Lewis did identify traits that do characterise people trapped in poverty in a number of different societies. However, the characteristics he attributed to cultural factors are in fact adaptations to structural inequalities. Thus, the theory was never relevant to Irish Travellers or any Travellers for a number of reasons which I will now identify.

In the first place, economic poverty is not the central issue as far as Travellers are concerned. Every economic level can be found among Irish Travellers ranging from small groups of wealthy families to groups of very poor families. This is an important fact because it demonstrates the viability of the Traveller way of life despite the serious structural obstacles it faces.

Secondly, Traveller culture is not a sub-culture of Irish society but a culture in its own right which has more in common with Gypsies, Travellers and economic nomads worldwide than it has with settled people of any nationality. Travellers identify with each other across national boundaries and divide the world into Traveller and non-Traveller, Gypsy and gadje.

Thirdly, the sub-culture of poverty theory does not deal with the issue of nomadism. Nomadism, however, is central to the understanding of Travellers and of their way of life and their relationship with the settled society.

Finally, the issues of separate language, separate norms and value systems are not addressed by the sub-cultural theory. I will now look at each of these points in more detail.

Economic Poverty

Irish Travellers, in common with Travellers everywhere, are basically economic nomads. The economic base of Traveller society is the family or the extended family and a wide range of economic activities, which serve the settled communities, have historically been carried out by them.

The Traveller community includes groups of families, often referred to as traders, very successful economically, who work at Traveller occupations within the traditional Traveller structure of the extended family. Although numerically a small minority, they represent an important role model for all Travellers. Most young Travellers aspire to the lifestyle of the so-called traders and not to that of the settled population, as most policy makers seem to believe.

Very many Irish Travellers are economically poor and indeed some are almost destitute. However, they are not a homogeneous group economically and practically all Travellers aspire to be economically independent at specific Traveller enterprises.

The Travellers' work pattern is also very different from that of the settled population. They work as families in their own time beside their homes and do not work for other people, i.e. bosses. Most Irish Travellers still engage in some form of economic activity, however sporadic, even if the enterprise does not bring in much money.

Traveller women and children, too, have always had an economic role, including begging, dealing, fortune-telling etc. Travellers pride themselves on their ability to survive in circumstances that settled people could not survive in and to find ways of making a living in the most difficult environments. They are innovative and enterprising and this is a trait they share with other Gypsies and Travellers. However, their work consists almost exclusively of providing marginal services to the settled population.

Current policies operated by both the welfare system and the local authorities militate against Travellers' enterprising ability and represent a serious threat to their economic base and also, consequently, to their social structure.

A Separate Cultural Group

Irish Travellers identify themselves as a separate group within Irish society, but they are not a sub-cultural group. They are almost exclusively endogamous – that is they prefer to marry within the group. In fact, many Travellers, in common with all other Gypsy and Traveller groups, prefer to marry within the extended family. Status within Traveller society is ascribed, it cannot be achieved. This means that you have to be born a Traveller, you cannot become one.

All Travellers classify the world into Traveller and Non-Traveller, Gypsy and gadje. Irish Travellers share many cultural patterns and values with Gypsies and Travellers worldwide. The most important value is the absolutely dominant position of the family and the extended family. Early marriage, close kin marriage, patriarchy, respect for older members of the family, rituals surrounding death and marriage, work patterns, and the type of relationships with the dominant settled society are all cultural patterns which Travellers share across national boundaries. The dominant position of the stable, traditional patriarchal family differs very significantly from the supposedly unstable single parent families which Lewis identified as one of the traits of the sub-culture of poverty.

Travellers share a field of communications which is exclusive to their group. They are also subject to the same kinds of discrimination and racism in almost every country they live in. This racism, which ranges from the extermination of a quarter of a million Gypsies and Travellers by the Nazis to the institutionalised racism practised in this country, is in itself a clear demonstration of Travellers' separate identity and lifestyle. In fact, they have historically been considered so separate that a whole series of laws have been passed against their very existence in many European countries. There is a clear recognition on the part of the law-makers that Travellers do indeed have a separate group identity.

Nomadism

The issue of nomadism is central to the understanding of Traveller society. Nomadism remains an aspiration for the majority of Travellers even when they have lived in the same spot for many years or even all of their lives. Nomadism, the desire to travel, the economic need to travel, the right to travel, these issues are fundamental to the existence of Travellers' society. Travellers are economic nomads, providing marginal services to a generally hostile wider society.

The services they traditionally provided to a rural population were: tin-smithing, dealing in a variety of goods, seasonal farm labouring, entertaining, fortune-telling etc. When they had covered an area with their wares and services, they moved on to the next. The advent of plastic, mass communications, supermarkets and "the dole" have changed that situation and the lifestyle and culture of the Travellers has adapted but not fundamentally changed in response. Many Travellers still prefer to live in trailers, to travel around for at least the summer months, to move back and forward to England for example, to visit their kin, to try their luck somewhere else or simply to see other places and people.

Travellers' sense of identification with a place is different from that of settled people. They retain the ability and willingness to travel even if they have lived in houses for years. The children of housed Travellers frequently return to living in trailers and to travelling – a fact that annoys and amazes administrators and policy makers but which is perfectly logical from a Traveller point of view. Most Travellers retain their cultural identity no matter how long they have lived in houses and their children frequently become nomadic at least for a few years.

Their material culture, the trailers and the vans, facilitates their nomadism and are symbolically important, a fact that is frequently misinterpreted by the settled world. Travellers spend their money on what they can take with them when travelling and therefore a significant percent of their expenditure is on transport – cars and vans and specifically on the kind of transport that enables them to earn a living. Transport has a much higher priority and significance for Travellers, precisely because they are nomadic.

Unfortunately very few of the social services or the health or education services are prepared to recognise the nomadic nature of Traveller society, let alone adapt their services in response. Nomadism was not an issue at all in the writings of Oscar Lewis or in the sub-culture of poverty but it is a key concept in understanding Traveller society.

Language, Norms and Values

Travellers' language, Cant or Gammon, is still widely understood but not widely used nowadays. My impression is that a fairly restricted number of words and phrases are still in common usage. This is a secret language and it is designed to exclude Non-Travellers. Just how old it is is the subject of debate and research at present. The significant thing about the language, however, is its existence. It gives weight to the identification of Travellers as a separate ethnic group.

All other Gypsy and Traveller groups have their own language, some of which are dialects of a single language, such as the various dialects of Romany spoken by different Gypsy groups. Other European Traveller groups, such as the Sinti in Germany, have set up cultural centres where their language is taught to the youth by older members of the group in order to preserve it and to strengthen the sense of identity of the group. This would be a useful project for Irish Travellers, too, while their language is still spoken, even in a restricted way.

On the question of norms and values, it would require a separate paper to deal with all of the normative patterns and the value systems that are specific to Irish Travellers. The value system revolves around the central importance of the family and the extended family, the ability to survive economically and to be independent and the ability to travel and trade as the opportunity arises.

Norms include: early marriage, close kin marriage, specific rituals around death, ritual cleansing, how relationships between men and women are regulated, how conflict is handled within the group etc. In all of these areas and in several others, Traveller norms and values are quite different, quite separate from those of the settled population. This system of norms and values constitutes a cohesive, separate parallel cultural system.

The strength of the culture is demonstrated by its ability to withstand specific long-term policies in the fields of education and of housing and accommodation which were designed to assimilate Travellers into the wider society and to simply do away with their separate identity. There is no doubt that these policies have failed. There are more Travellers living a Traveller lifestyle in trailers now, for example, than there were at the time of the 1963 Report of the Commission on Itinerancy.

The vast majority of Irish Travellers have no interest whatsoever in losing their separate Traveller identity and culture and demonstrate this fact over and over again by simply not co-operating with policies or services which they perceive as a threat to their culture. They may not articulate their fears in such terms as these but they behave consistently in a way that protects their own value system.

The traits listed by Lewis as the sub-culture of poverty fell far short of a cohesive value and normative system. The sub-culture of poverty was much more an adaptation to difficult economic and social conditions and was defined by the relationship with the wider society. This is not the case for Irish Travellers whose culture exists in its own right and is in no way defined by its relationship with the settled society.

Wrong

CONCLUSION

In conclusion, the sub-culture of poverty theory has nothing to offer Irish Travellers as an explanation for their existence or their lifestyle. It has done them a great disservice in so far as the theory has been used by certain people to discredit Travellers and to negate their separate cultural identity.

As a mono-cultural society, we have serious difficulties adjusting to the idea that there is another equally valid culture in existence in this society. Multi-cultural approaches in education and other sevices are the norm now in many European countries and they need to be taken on board here seriously to accommodate Travellers' needs in a culturally valid way. There is simply no other way to make any progress in improving Travellers' physical and social conditions or to address the serious issues of racism and discrimination which they face as a group.

REFERENCES

Acton, Thomas   *Gypsy Politics and Social Change.* London: Routledge and Kegan Paul, 1974.

Commission on Itinerancy   *Report of the Commission on Itinerancy.* Dublin: The Stationery Office, 1963.

Gmelch, Sharon   *Tinkers and Travellers, Ireland's Nomads.* Dublin: O'Brien Press, 1975.

Lewis, O.   "The Culture of Poverty", *Scientific American*, Vol. 215, No. 4, October 1966, 19-25.

Lewis, O.   *La Vida.* London: Panther Books, 1965.

Liégeois, Jean Pierre   *Gypsies and Travellers.* Council of Europe, 1985.

McCarthy, Patricia   *Itinerancy and Poverty: a Study in the Sub-Culture of Poverty.* Unpublished M.Soc.Sc. Thesis. Dublin: University College, 1972.

Valentine, C.   *Culture and Poverty.* Chicago: University of Chicago Press, 1968.

THE SUB-CULTURE OF POVERTY —
A RESPONSE TO McCARTHY

Martin Collins

As a Traveller I welcome Patricia McCarthy's refutation of her earlier study, carried out in Galway nearly twenty years ago, in which she argues for the utility of the sub-culture of poverty theory for understanding Irish Travellers (see Chapter 8). It takes courage to admit that one has made mistakes and to develop new analyses when the old theories fail to explain situations adequately. This is particularly important when the lives of other people are affected by the policies based on these theories. This raises a general point about academics and research which I would like to make before responding to McCarthy's contribution to this volume.

For too long Travellers have been unaware of the theories that have been constructed about them and have not been in a position to evaluate or judge these theories. Because of this we have been used to some extent by people who have researched our way of life and in the process become established as "experts". It is not good enough that Travellers should be the objects of other people's research. This does not mean that I am against research, not at all, but academics have a responsibility at least to make their findings known to us and accessible to more Travellers. In this way we can judge for ourselves whether we think the conclusions drawn are accurate and see what the implications are for policies.

The importance of this is obvious when we consider the sub-culture of poverty theory. It is hard to prove the connection between theory and practice and many of the people implementing policies do not admit to having any particular theory. They see themselves as doing a job or solving a number of problems, and theory may seem very remote from this. However, when they are questioned about their practice or challenged about the policies being implemented they do sometimes admit to holding certain theoretical views about Travellers. For example, when social workers are questioned about the way they relate to Travellers they may acknowledge that they do not see Travellers as an ethnic group but as a sub-culture of poverty. Likewise, when the local authorities are challenged about the way they set out to "distribute the problem" (i.e. Travellers) evenly among the different electoral areas, or the ways they try to stop Travellers from travelling or collecting scrap, they sometimes admit that they do not recognise Travellers as having a distinct cultural identity. Even though the sub-culture of poverty theory has been refuted, many officials and people working with Travellers still use it as a justification for their actions and policies.

According to the sub-culture of poverty theory, as applied to Travellers, poverty and deprivation are self-perpetuating and Traveller children are conditioned into this way of life.They then develop backward attitudes and values which correspond to this poor way of life and which prevent them from developing socially and economically. The false assumption here is that all Travellers are economically poor. As Patricia McCarthy points out there is a whole range of economic levels within the Traveller community. However, when the local authorities come across wealthy Travellers who do not fit the poverty stereotype they refuse to call them Travellers, referring to them as "traders" and setting up a false division between true and false Travellers.

Of course, many Travellers are living in poverty and are forced to become dependent on the state. The sub-culture of poverty theorists blame Travellers for this situation and places the main responsibility for the poverty on Travellers rather than on the structures of inequality which exist. Travellers living in poor circumstances do sometimes become apathetic and fatalistic but many others manage to struggle not only for survival but to improve their situation. They do not resign themselves to accepting their situation. In fact, it would be interesting to compare a group of Travellers with a group of settled people living in similar circumstances. I think Travellers might be the ones to show initiative and creativity in finding ways to improve their situation. There is evidence for this in the way Travellers have adjusted to the changes which took place in the economy, which wiped out their traditional crafts and trades. Travellers developed new ways and adapted to the changes taking place in the wider society. In doing this they also retained a strong sense of their own identity.

I referred earlier to a new and growing awareness among Travellers. This new awareness is about having a clear understanding of the reasons for the differences between Travellers and settled people. These differences are cultural and do not mean being either inferior or superior – just different but equal. More Travellers are rejecting the culture of poverty theory and the policies and practices which follow from it because we see ourselves as a distinct ethnic group. This enables us to put into words, and to have concepts which explain, our experiences and what has been happening to us. There are important implications from this. It means that we can be clearer about our rights and that we can be confident in making demands. It means, for example, that, in order for Travellers to benefit from the educational system, it isn't just Travellers who have to change but also the schooling system itself that has to be adjusted to ensure that Travellers can be catered for in a way that is appropriate. Likewise for other state services. We need to examine these to ensure that the way these services are structured and delivered is not excluding Travellers.

In rejecting this culture of poverty theory Travellers are calling for a society which acknowledges diversity. Surely this is a positive and enriching thing. What amazes me is the resistance to this. What is the reason for the fear and the resistance when we look for space to have different cultures existing side-by-side? I would be interested in hearing an explanation for this.

I welcome Patricia McCarthy's contribution and hope that it is read by all those who have been operating out of the theory she refutes. More importantly, I hope that it will influence policy makers so that they will rethink the basis for their actions in a way which respects Travellers' cultural identity.

TRAVELLERS' LANGUAGE:
A SOCIOLINGUISTIC PERSPECTIVE

Alice Binchy

The 25,000 Travellers in Ireland all speak a language spoken by no one who does not belong to their group. Irish Travellers in Britain and North America speak the same language. This language is not taught in schools, even all-Traveller ones; it is not written in books that Travellers have access to; it is not heard on radio, television or in plays or films. The academic name for the language is Shelta, but Travellers call it Gammon or Cant. I use the term Shelta because it is accepted academically, and also as a cover term for both Cant and Gammon. In its present form, it consists of a vocabulary which is used in a somewhat simplified English grammatical structure. Much of the vocabulary consists of Irish words which have been transformed or disguised, using a number of regular changes. Children generally learn the language in infancy, as a joint first language, and they are told not to tell outsiders anything about the language.

The language is used by Travellers among their own community, and in the presence of settled people in a variety of situations. Children use it among themselves when they attend settled schools; it is used in shops, welfare and unemployment offices, doctors' surgeries, clinics and hospitals; in police stations, courtrooms and prisons, both between prisoners of Traveller origin and between prisoners and their visitors; it is used on public transport, buses and trains within Ireland and on ferries between Ireland and England. All of these contexts have one thing in common: Travellers as a secret compressed enclave in a settled world.

Shelta first came to light in the 1880s, when Charles Leland, in *The Gypsies* (1882), told of coming across an Irish Traveller in Britain who mentioned another language that was far older than Romani and was habitually spoken by Irish tinkers, as they were then called. The language was called Shelta or Sheldhru, and Leland in his excitement described it as a fifth Celtic language, maybe even the lost language of the Picts. When Leland published news of his discovery, which came at a time of great upsurge of interest in the Gypsy/Traveller way of life, many amateur folklore collectors were galvanised into action, and before long the pages of the Journal of the Gypsy Lore Society were filled with sightings of Irish Travellers, and specimens of their language. Although it was accepted that the language "belonged" to Irish Travellers, and was not related to Romani, most of the interest in the Travellers' language was outside Ireland itself: only one short vocabulary came from Co. Wexford. Most of the early material consisted of simple wordlists, and, since few of the collectors had any knowledge of Irish, Irish words were frequently included mistakenly in the lists. One of the early collectors, however, Crofton (1886), knew enough Irish to be able to recognise that some Shelta words were formed by the application of disguise rules to Irish words, e.g.:

Shelta	Irish	English
rodas	doras	door
laicin	cailín	girl
tobar	bóthar	road

Academic interest in the language began when John Sampson of the University of Liverpool, and the German folklorist and scholar Kuno Meyer, took up the study of the language. Both of these believed that the language was very old, and they based this on three main facts: (i) archaic words were preserved in Shelta, sometimes in disguised form, words which had previously been known only from old manuscripts, e.g. the Shelta word *cuinne* "a priest" is an old word for a druid (Sampson 1891); (ii) some of the methods of disguising words in Shelta were identical to those employed in monastic manuscripts of ancient times, by monks who wanted to preserve some material in secrecy; (iii) some words seemed to have been formed from pre-aspirated or lenited Irish, e.g. the Irish words *bothar* and *lamh* became, respectively, *tobar* and *malya* in Shelta, rather than *hobar and *valya, as they would have been had Modern Irish been the source. Sampson and Meyer suggested that these words, and others, might have been taken into Shelta before the rule of lenition became established in Irish phonology, which was before the twelfth century (Thurneysen 1961).

Although Sampson and Meyer both published several papers on Shelta, the definitive work on the language was written by R.A.S. Macalister, as a chapter of *The Secret Languages of Ireland* (1937). This was published after Sampson's death, and was a compilation of all the previously published work on Shelta. Macalister, unlike Sampson and Meyer, believed that the language was of recent origin, that it had been formed by people who were predominantly English-speaking, who had been aided in its construction by educated people: this explained (to his satisfaction) the inclusion of material from early manuscript sources. Macalister may be criticised on many fronts, but the criticism most relevant to what I have to say is that he saw Travellers ("Tinkers") as an occupational group, even though earlier collectors had described the language as spoken by chimney-sweeps, knife-grinders, sieve-makers, flower-sellers, hawkers, pedlars and other vagrants. Macalister regarded Shelta as an occupational argot or jargon, spoken by members of an occupational group in the course of their work.

A SECRET LANGUAGE?

Shelta has been described as a secret language, but this term is rather misleading. It is a secret language in the sense that few people other than its speakers know of its existence, but the term is more often used to describe the jargon of groups who have something to hide. Market traders who want to communicate with each other in front of customers, petty criminals in front of their victims, doctors and lawyers in front of their patients or clients,all feel the need to communicate with members of their own group in an exclusive way. The difference is that these are all occupational groups, and Travellers, although they have gravitated towards certain specific occupations, are not an occupational group. Okely (1983, 67) lists preference for self-employment (along with nomadism, language and rituals of cleanliness) as one of the cultural values by which Travellers and Gypsies identify themselves.

If one asks Travellers today when the language is used, one is invariably told that it is used in the presence of settled people, when Travellers want to communicate with each other and do not want outsiders to hear. But very often the messages passed in this way have no "secret" content at all, e.g. statements such as *I'm corribed with the krolus* (I'm killed with the hunger). Travellers say that this type of communication is aided by the fact that Shelta is interspersed with English words, so that the casual listener does not realise that another language is being used. It is quite hard to get Travellers to admit that they use Shelta when outsiders are not present – not because they want to deceive the enquirer, but because they genuinely do not realise that they use Shelta habitually in some set circumstances. This is common in speakers of dialects, whose self-reportage of language use is notoriously unreliable (Fasold 1984). Again, this is not because they wish to deceive but because language choice in unguarded conversation is a largely unconscious process; and also because differences in status between dialect and standard varieties mean that self-esteem is better served by a conviction that one is a standard speaker. The range of the Shelta lexicon, as well as direct fieldwork evidence, are indicators that Shelta has a wider usage than was previously thought.

Older Travellers are jealous of the secrecy of Shelta – they do not want it known, and with few exceptions, they do not want it recorded. I believe that the issue of secrecy is closely bound up with Travellers' view of themselves, and their place in society. This can be compared with the frequently-reported statements of creole and patois speakers who say that their creole or patois doesn't exist, and that they wouldn't speak it if it did. Many Travellers fear that, if settled people got hold of the language, they would use it to humiliate Travellers. There is a constant fear that the Gárdaí are trying to pick up the language, not only for the purpose of eaves-dropping on Travellers in custody, but as an added weapon of ridicule. One young Traveller told me of a visit to a Traveller friend in prison, where the prison guard, knowing them to be Travellers, at the end of visiting time said *Crush on laicin, time to misli,* "Come on, girl, time to go." This was taken by both Travellers as a jibe at the notion that Travellers consider themselves different from the majority.

SHELTA AND IDENTITY

The relationship between Shelta and the Travellers' sense of ethnic identity is a complex one. Travellers were defined as an ethnic group by Gmelch and Gmelch (1976), but it seems that this designation came about because they thought the term subculture was too pejorative. It is the Gmelchs' view that Traveller ethnicity developed over a relatively short period. When the source of free accommodation for Travel-lers in the barns and outhouses of friendly farmers dried up in the 1880s, Travellers were forced to construct dwellings of their own, in tents and later wagons. The Gmelchs' argument is that the development of a separate material culture led to the growth of a separate ethnicity. This begs quite a lot of questions, mainly concerning the language. It is notable that the Gmelchs designate the language a "secret argot", with the implications of antisocial behaviour that this connotes. They do not seem to have considered the ideology of nomadism as an element in Traveller culture. If Travellers were basically the same as settled people until the 1880s, differing only in not having permanent accommodation of their own, why did they need a "secret argot"? How did they recognise each other? How could they tell who was a Traveller and who a vagrant? How could a Traveller from one end of the country understand the Shelta of another from the opposite end?

One cannot become a Traveller. People who live in caravans or mobile homes do not become Travellers; and Travellers who live in houses do not become settled people. Only those who have at least one Traveller parent are accepted as Travellers; people who marry Travellers are not accepted as Travellers, although their children are. Travellers can opt out of the Traveller community, and into the settled community, but settled people cannot become Travellers. Travellers can become part of the settled community only by leaving behind their Traveller identity: and there is some evidence that Travellers are reluctant to do this.

In 1969 Jared Harper, of the University of Georgia, U.S.A., wrote an M.A. thesis on the Cant spoken by a community of Irish Travellers who left Ireland between 1848-1850. Although the American Travellers have more money than Travellers here, they still live in extended family groups, often in settlements on land they have bought themselves, in trailers as well as in houses. They speak the same language as Irish Travellers: I have shown lists of Harper's words to Travellers here, and they have been instantly recognised. Why have these Travellers retained the Traveller language? If all they needed was a secret code, to use in the presence of settled Americans, then they could have used Irish.

It is the hallmark of the emigrant that he or she is ready to change or adapt, but most emigrants have a part of their identity that they are not willing to surrender to the melting pot, and these ethnic markers may be retained over generations. It is interesting to compare the ethnic markers retained by settled Irish emigrants to America at the same time. Many of the emigrants to America at the time of the Famine were Irish speaking (Ó Cuiv 1969), and the Irish language was retained for some time in America, where there were Irish-speaking ghettoes in some of the larger cities. As time went on, and the emigrants became predominantly English-speaking, they retained an interest in the Irish language. The Irish-American magazine carried an occasional column in Irish from 1857, and in 1873, the Philo-Celtic society of Boston was formed, to promote the Irish language, traditional music and dancing and publications in Irish (Kallen 1984). This is the common pattern of emigrants everywhere, who fix on part of their culture as worthy symbols of their different ethnicity.

If we look at the group of Traveller emigrants, it is clear that the ethnic markers they retained are significantly different from those of the settled Irish. When they first arrived, they settled in upstate New York, around Pittsburgh, and in Washington D.C., but they found the winters too cold for their outdoor way of life and after the Civil War they moved south, where they specialised in trading horses and mules. The mule trade declined early in this century, and the Travellers diversified into dealing, door-to-door, in carpets and linoleum, and spray-painting barns (Harper and Hudson 1971). In Ireland also, when farm animal trading declined, and plastic replaced tinware, Travellers diversified into other trades. These included selling carpets door-to-door and, while there is no tradition of spray-painting barns, laying tarmac driveways for suburban residents seems a related occupation. The preference for self-employment is more characteristic of Travellers than any specific trade.

The Georgia Travellers retained the language they brought with them to America. The same Shelta or Cant words have American English equivalents in America and Hiberno-English equivalents in Ireland, e.g. *sheydogue* is given by Harper as meaning a sheriff, while Travellers here say it means a guard. The few regional differences between the Georgia Cant and that spoken here can be easily worked out by Travellers used to Shelta word formations, e.g. the American Cant word *grandy* for candy. The difference in ethnic markers retained by Travellers and settled Irish is convincing evidence that Travellers have a different ethnicity, and that their language is an ethnic language.

IDENTITY AND LINGUISTIC STRATEGIES

I want now to look in more detail at reasons why Travellers remain Travellers, and also at some of the linguistic strategies adopted by groups whose internal integrity is threatened, for instance as a result of emigration. I am arguing that Travellers' internal integrity is under threat as they come under increased pressure to assimilate to the settled way of life. Travellers, at present, could be compared to refugees, unsure of whether they are going to be able to adapt and unwilling to jettison anything from the old way of life until they are certain that a better alternative is offered. Linguistically, it is not so much a case of learning a new language as transposing the restricted language used in their dealings with the majority into an expanded range of contexts. For emigrants, language sometimes acquires a new emotional value as an aspect of their ethnic identity. Ingram (1979) distinguishes between learning about a language, and learning a language. The former involves learning enough to make oneself understood, the latter learning to use the language in context, and becoming aware of the complicated semiotic patterns which constitute the culture of its speakers. I would argue that Travellers take the first approach with regard to English.

There are several possible responses to language contact. One is identity transfer, where the learner's old culture is abandoned to achieve membership of the new group. A language shift usually follows. Another is identity defence, which involves avoidance of the majority group and language as a strategy for protecting one's own group identity. The identity defence response may involve considerable social and economic disadvantages for those who choose it (Crawford 1987). There are undoubted economic disadvantages to remaining Travellers, but the social drawbacks may be visible only from the settled side of the fence: as Northover says "groups who may be ascribed a low status in their host society nevertheless retain a strong and positive evaluation of themselves and their own group, since they are able to distinguish between alter-ascribed identity of the stereotyped kind and their own perception of themselves" (Northover 1984, 185–6).

Taylor and others (Taylor 1980; Giles and Johnson 1981; Taylor and McKirnan 1984) looked at language contact from the point of view of ethnic groups in contact situations, using a dynamic model which has some applications to the Travellers' situation. The model involves a progression through stages which may endure only briefly or over generations, depending on the power and status of the groups involved.

Stage 1 is where the disadvantaged group is in a stable hierarchical relationship with the power group, and they accept their low status as a reflection of their true worth. If the group want to progress socially, they will have to conform to the dominant culture. Members generally acquire a working knowledge of the dominant language, but native-like speech is not expected of them or aspired to by them.

In Stage 2, inferior status is still attributed internally, but the more ambitious of the group try to avoid negative aspects of the group's status by abandoning it in favour of the dominant culture. Native-like proficiency in the dominant language is seen as the key to a rise in status. This stage of development is usually supported by the educational system, and the maintenance of both cultures is seen as transitional, leading to a whole-hearted transfer of identity. In Stage 3, those who are unwilling or unable to assimilate stop attributing their low status internally, and begin protesting about the injustices of the system. They will concentrate on the internal status of the group, and on mobilising support for a more positive social identity. Linguistically, this leads to an emphasis on the ethnic language. Stage 4 involves social competition and will follow if group members have a strong group identity and see their group's status as unfair and unstable. Ethnic groups in this situation try politically to change the status quo. They may go on to demand recognition of their language as appropriate for public as well as private discourse and to demand separate educational facilities, which, in fact, may be essential if ethnic groups are not destined for eventual assimilation.

With regard to Travellers, it is clear that across the spectrum of Traveller life there are individuals and small groups at every stage of this model, with the possible exception of Stage 4. What settled people might regard as the average Traveller, illiterate, with a life expectancy of 50 years, camped illegally at the side of the road, is certainly at Stage 1 : grateful, at least outwardly, for whatever society chooses to give him, and not expecting any concessions to be made to the notion of a distinctive Traveller culture. It seems likely that the secrecy of Shelta, the fact that Travellers deny its existence to any but the most determined enquirer, is linked to this perception of their place in society.

It is interesting to note where agencies helping Travellers locate themselves on the scale. The original Itinerant Settlement Commission, set up in the early 1960s, came in at Stage 2, with the avowed aim of assimilating Travellers into the settled community:

"it is not considered that there is any alternative to a positive drive for housing itinerants, if a permanent solution to the problem of itinerancy, based on absorption and integration, is to be achieved" (Report of the Commission on Itinerancy 1963, 62).

Later bodies, notably the Dublin Travellers Education and Development Group (DTEDG), came in at Stage 3, running personal development courses for young Travellers, training them to speak publicly on behalf of all Travellers, and to challenge the injustices of the system. This group has also worked to develop a more positive attitude to the Travellers' language, which was in danger of being discarded by those Travellers, perhaps at earlier developmental stages, who considered the language something to be ashamed of.

It is fair to say that Travellers have not yet reached Stage 4. Travellers' claim to ethnic status will not be accepted until the mainstream population is convinced, by Travellers themselves, that their claim is legitimate; and Travellers will not perceive that their position in society is illegitimate until they collectively assert the value of their culture including language as proof of a different ethnicity.

Discarding their language and culture as the price of admission to full participation in settled society is the only option open to Travellers at present. The previous treatment of Shelta has ensured that its use will be seen as divisive, since it has been treated as a secret language to be used against settled people. Travellers are seen as deviant members of the majority culture. Their culture, including language, is viewed as existing primarily in the eyes of sympathetic settled people, people who are frequently accused of "telling Travellers that they're different". Travellers do not need to be told that they are different. It is not so much that Irish society is not tolerant of diversity, although that could be said, but rather that the particular type of diversity that Travellers epitomise is considered illegitimate. Some commentators (e.g. Rigal 1989) think that Travellers' cultural distinctiveness will be submerged in the near future, as the price of integration into mainstream society: Travellers, it is argued, are coming to the conclusion that nomadism is no longer possible. This view implies that Traveller culture and distinctiveness is a transitory manifestation of a downtrodden, outlawed position in society. The view of Shelta as a secret language to be used against settled people is a direct outgrowth of this.

PIDGIN AND CREOLE LANGUAGES

The restrictions both in form and function of Shelta have led it to be compared to pidgin and creole languages (Hancock 1974; Seaholm 1977). Pidgin languages come about when two groups speaking different languages have to communicate for some specific purpose. They were common by-products of the slave trade, where slave owners were careful to mix slaves of different origins, to prevent sedition. The simplest definition of a pidgin is that it takes the vocabulary of one language and the grammar of another: this is one reason why Shelta, which uses some disguised Irish words as vocabulary, and the grammar of English, was compared to pidgins. Pidgins are languages stripped of all but the barest necessities for communication: they are born of the need to communicate without any of the supports of a shared background. Shelta is different in that it serves to communicate between those who share a background. A major point of similarity is that between the increased motivation to communicate which causes pidgins to develop in situations of mutual need, and the increased motivation to communicate exclusively with their own community felt by an outcast group in what they perceive as a hostile environment. Both situations, apparently, bring similar strategies into play.

In normal communication between speakers of the same language, the message itself is only part of what is communicated. The grammar and style in which messages are put carry social information which can be decoded by those who speak the language as natives. When speakers of different languages have to communicate, complex grammatical and syntactical relationships in their native languages are discarded, since the social meanings they carry are no longer relevant. In the case of Travellers, those parts of the standard language which carry only socially relevant information are redundant to a small closed speech community which is outside that of the standard language speakers. In pidgin situations, nonverbal language, gestures and so on, and clues from the context combine to fill the gap left by grammar, and the same is true, to a certain extent, of Shelta.

The process of creolization usually comes about when children are born into a pidgin-speaking community. For the parents, the pidgin is a second language: when the circumstances which produced the pidgin persist long enough for a second generation to be born, the pidgin, which is the children's first language, develops in their mouths into a creole. Creoles are different from pidgins in that they are not reduced in form and function: they develop grammatical and syntactical structures of their own, and they serve the same range of functions as any other first language. The question that might be asked is why this has not happened in the case of Shelta, which certainly has been around long enough to have had many generations coming across it as a first language.

Pidgins that become creolized do so because the range of contexts in which a pidgin is used expands when it becomes a first language. With Shelta, because the social position of Travellers has not changed over the centuries, the language has not been allowed to spread into other contexts of use. The situation can be compared to that of British Black English speakers, who are immigrants to Britain from the West

Indies (Edwards 1986). In the West Indies, Black people are the majority population, and they have access to all levels of the social hierarchy; and their use of standard English and patois or creole forms a continuous system. In Britain, on the other hand, Black people are restricted in their access to high-status jobs, and their two alternative ways of speaking remain separate systems. The restrictions in Travellers' social position may have prevented creolization: on the other hand, this may be one of the reasons why Shelta has survived. Hancock (1989) has suggested that social oppression may be one of the reasons why the Romani language has survived.

Shelta may be described as being functionally reduced. Functions here refer to the communicative purposes to which a language is put. These include the propositional or referential function, which is the message itself, and information which has a truth value; the directive function, which means language used to get things done; the integrative function, language used for solidarity and to signal group membership; and the expressive function, which refers to personal feelings towards either the message or the speaker. First language development begins with integrative and directive functions: the mother teaching her baby to talk does not begin with propositions like "The sun rises in the east", but rather with things like "Who's my best baby?" Baby talk has an integrative function. Pidgins develop the propositional function first because they are not used for intimate contact. The integrative function is fulfilled by pidgin speakers' first language. In the case of Travellers, where all communication with outsiders is in the propositional or referential mode, and all communication with their own group can include Shelta, it can be argued that their use of Hiberno-English is pidgin-like. Speaking to outsiders is the only context where Shelta is never used.

Pidgins are usually learned by adults, which explains why the referential function is important. Shelta, in contrast, is learned in infancy, so that integrative and expressive functions appear earlier. The developmental hierarchy of functions for Shelta is similar to that of a first language, rather than a pidgin. Muhlhausler (1986:87) described the different environmental surroundings of a first language and a pidgin in the following terms:

"Whereas a first language develops in the social security of parent-child interaction and eventually enables the child to relate to the world outside, pidgin speakers are faced first with a hostile and dangerous world, and only gradually do they develop the structural and functional means to make that world a home".

Travellers are aware of the hostile and dangerous world outside their own community from infancy, and Shelta is part of their response to it. The expressive function appears in statements of personal feelings by Travellers in the hostile and dangerous world, e.g. *Galyune, I'm anshif, I'm all lagadi and the nidyas are suni-in at me* "I'm embarrassed, I'm all dirty and the people are looking at me". The speaker expresses her feelings to members of her own community: this is not secret communication. The expressive and the integrative functions are closely linked in Shelta since both have the effect of drawing comfort from the fact of belonging to a close-knit community. The directive function, which is also developmentally early in first languages, appears to be important in organising the Traveller community's interaction with the outside world, e.g. planning strategies for begging: *Geig alamch aidh, and I'll geig a milc of durra* "(You) ask for buttermilk, and I'll ask for a bit of bread".

The most important functions of Shelta appear to be integrative, expressive and directive. All could in fact be subsumed under the integrative function, since they are all concerned with maintaining and reinforcing the boundaries of the Traveller community against incursions from the settled world. Travellers' dealings directly with settled people, through Hiberno-English, are functionally reduced, since they have no expressive or integrative content at all, merely propositional.

Reductions in function lead to reductions in form. One of the supposed similarities between Shelta and pidgin languages is that Shelta apparently takes its vocabulary from one source and its grammar from another: many of the words come from Irish, and are Sheltified by a regular system of changes; and the grammar is that of Hiberno-English, albeit in a somewhat simplified form. It should perhaps be said at this point that the fact that Shelta seems to have no independent grammar does not mean that it cannot be described as a language. Hindi and Urdu in India, Bokmal and Nynorsk in Norway, are recognized in law as distinct languages yet their grammars are almost identical. The reason they are recognized as distinct languages is because they are spoken by groups which are recognized as distinct ethnically (Wardhaugh 1987; Haugen 1966). Definitions of what is and what is not a language are based on social and political, rather than purely linguistic, factors. Shelta has the misfortune to find itself in close proximity to two languages whose prestige has been established, linguistically, for centuries, namely Irish and English. An unwritten, unstandardised, unknown language, spoken by a stigmatized group, has an unenviable task when it seeks admittance to the class of language, because of generally held assumptions, both implicit and explicit, about what a language is.

Why has Shelta no apparent grammar of its own? There are several possible answers. One is that constant switching between Shelta and Hiberno-English has caused two separate grammars to converge, leaving only differences of vocabulary: this is what happened in the Indian village of Kupwar, as reported by Gumperz and Wilson (1971). There is another possible explanation which I will offer now. I want to examine the relationship between the Traveller community and its language, with illustrations from the growth of creole communities. The central point I want to make is that the present state of Shelta may be explained by the tradition of travelling and living in small family groups.

LANGUAGE, COMMUNITY AND NOMADISM

It seems fairly obvious that for language to develop, there has to be some unity of purpose. In the case of pidgins, which develop where there has been no common language, there is agreement on both sides about the need to communicate, albeit in a very basic way. Pidgins are culture-neutral, since they aim to cross cultural boundaries. They eliminate grammatical features which would convey only social information to members of the same speech community. Creoles, on the other hand, develop from a combination of cultural and environmental factors. Cultural environment is not only the trigger, but also a constituent in the growth of grammar.

When a pidgin develops, all the strategies adopted by its speakers are geared towards ease of communication across cultural and linguistic barriers. Grammar is not necessary for efficient communication. When pidgins develop into creoles and become the language of a closed communication network, they use grammatical devices to categorise members into social groups. Grammar becomes a means of signalling membership and relative status.

For grammar to develop, the established thinking is that there has to be community (Muhlhausler 1986; LePage and Tabouret-Keller 1985). LePage (1977) suggests that grammar does not develop until or unless creole speakers commit an "act of identity" by which they identify their language as the language of a community. Close daily interaction leads a community's use of language to become focussed, meaning that individual solutions are replaced by rule-based grammar. The more interaction there is among a community, the more prescriptive their grammatical, as well as social, rules will be. The existence of a community is necessary for the development of grammatical rules.

The term "community" as used in sociolinguistics usually has as a primary feature "shared location". Shared location is an integral part of some of the best known sociolinguistic studies, e.g. Labov's study of Martha's Vineyard (1963), or Milroy's work in Belfast (1980). Both of these make a strong link between shared location, a sense of community and shared linguistic features. The question now is, whether there can be the same sense of community without shared location, and what are the consequences for language if there is no shared location. The sociolinguistic definition of community is, it seems, weighted in favour of sedentary societies. While other ethnic, racial or occupational groups can if they wish live in community together, this option, both by definition and by the way the norms of settled society impinge on them, is not open to those who describe themselves as Travellers. It is clear, however, that although they live and travel in small family groups, all Travellers owe allegiance to the greater "community" of Travellers. Travellers use Shelta as a social measuring-scale to locate unknown or unrelated Travellers, because, as one Traveller said, "it gives a better acceptance". Travellers do not live together as a community – the nature of their society (extended family groups) and their prefer-ence in terms of living accommodation (mobile rather than fixed) interact to make living in a community impossible.

Nmalism,

Travelling, nomadism, is woven into the very fabric of Traveller life. Travellers choose the occupations they do be-cause they are nomadic. Nomadism, moving, affects all as-pects of Traveller life, even death. The standard way of com-ing to terms with a bereavement is to move away from memo-

Dickie

ries of the dead person. The attitude to property is coloured by it: Travellers have little interest in material things for their own sake, only as readily realizable assets, to be disposed of ready for a new start after a move. Human relations are regulated by it – interfamilial conflict is resolved by moving away (Gmelch 1975). Even sexual morality is affected by it: many families will not stay near those whose morals they doubt, and youthful romances unlikely to lead to marriage are broken up by moving away.

Q ✱

Nomadism is one of the ways by which small Traveller groups retain faith with the larger Traveller community. It is the reason why some Travellers would willingly live all their lives in a caravan in one spot, but would not live in a house in the same spot. Travelling itself is not as important as remain-ing disposed to travel. The social setting of Shelta is small family groups, nomadic islands in a sedentary sea, signalling to each other across that sea, and united by the collection of habits and dispositions that is Traveller culture. The hypoth-esis is that the dispersion caused by nomadic habits has caused the language to develop as it has: that the small scale of Travellers' daily interactions with their own group was not enough to maintain Shelta grammmar. In the present system, lexicon is the ethnic marker, and grammar represents the parts of life shared with settled society.

Shelta uses a reduced form of English grammar because Travellers do not share a sense of community with settled people. Travellers in Ireland are seen as monolingual, and in their dealings with settled people they are judged on the basis of a restricted code. Within their own community they use Shelta, which, as I have shown, has restrictions of its own. But a distinction should be made between the restriction in Shelta, because of what need not be said, and the restriction in the code used to settled people, because of what cannot be said.

REFERENCES

Crawford, J.

"Identity, Speech Accommodation Theory and Second Language Learning in a Multicultural Society", *Revue de Phonetique Apliquée* 82-83-84, 1987.

Crofton, N.T.

"Shelta, the Tinkers' Language", *The Academy*, 18 Dec. 1886, p.412.

Edwards, V.

Language in a Black Community. Clevedon: Multilingual Matters, 1986.

Fasold, R.

The Sociolinguistics of Society. Oxford: Basil Blackwell, 1984.

Giles, H. and Johnson, P.

"The Role of Language in Ethnic Group Relations", in *Intergroup Behaviour.* J.C.Turner & H.Giles (eds). Oxford: Basil Blackwell, 1981.

Gmelch, G.

"Irish Traveller Sex Roles and Marriage Patterns", in *Gypsies, Tinkers and Other Travellers.* F.Rehfisch (ed.). London: Academic Press, 1975.

Gmelch, G. and Gmelch, S.

"The Emergence of an Ethnic Group", *Anthropological Quarterly*, 49, 1976, 225-38.

Gumperz, J. and Wilson, R.   "Convergence and Creolization: a Case from the Indo-Aryan/Dravidian Border", in *Pidginization and Creolization of Languages.* D.Hymes (ed.). Cambridge: Cambridge University Press, 1971.

Hancock, I.F.   "Shelta: A Problem of Classification", in *Pidgins and Creoles: Current Trends and Prospects.* P.deCamp and I.Hancock. Washington: Georgetown University Press, 1974.

"The Romani Speech Community", in *Silent Minorities.* V.Edwards & S.Alladina (eds). London: Longmans, 1989.

Harper, J   "Irish Traveler Cant: An Historical, Structural and Sociolinguistic Study of an Argot". Master's Thesis, University of Georgia, 1969.

Harper, J. and Hudson, C.   "Irish Traveler Cant", *Journal of English Linguistics 15.* 1971, 78-86.

Ingram, D.E.   "Aspects of Personality Development for Bilingualism". Paper delivered at *R.E.L.C. Regional Seminar on Acquisition of Bilingual Ability and Patterns of Bilingualism.* Singapore, April 1979, 16-21.

Kallen, J.   "Language and Ethnic Identity: The Irish Language in the United States", in *Language Across Cultures.* L. MacMathúna & D.Singleton (eds.). Dublin: Irish Association for Applied Linguistics, 1984.

Labov, W.   "The Social motivation of a Sound Change", *Word* 19, 1963, 273-309.

Leland, C.G.   "A Prehistoric Language yet Surviving in Britain", *The Academy,* 759, Nov. 20, 1886, 346.

"Shelta", *Journal of the Gypsy Lore Society.* 11: 1891, 321-323.

LePage, R. and Tabouret-Keller, A.   *Acts of Identity.* Cambridge: Cambridge University Press, 1985.

LePage, R.   "Processes of Pidginisation and
                            Creolization", in *Pidgin and Creole Linguis-
                            tics*. A. Valdman (ed.). Bloomington:
                            Indiana University Press, 1977.

Macalister, R.A.S.   *The Secret Languages of Ireland*. Cambridge:
                            Cambridge University Press, 1937.

Meyer, K.   "On the Irish Origin and the Age of Shelta",
                            Journal of the Gypsy Lore Society, 2. 1891,
                            257-66.

Milroy, L.   *Language and Social Networks*. Oxford: Basil
                            Blackwell, 1980.

Muhlhausler, P.   *Pidgin and Creole Linguistics*. Oxford: Basil
                            Blackwell, 1986.

Ní Shúinéar, S.   Commentary on MacAlister. Unpublished
                            manuscript, 1979.

Northover, M.   "Young Punjabi Bilinguals in Northern
                            Ireland: their Language Competence and
                            Identity Structure", in *Language Across Cul-
                            tures*. L. MacMathúna and D.Singleton
                            (eds.). Dublin: IRAAL, 1984, 171-193.

Ó Cuív, B.   *A View of the Irish Language*. Dublin: Station-
                            ery Office, 1969.

Okely, J.   *The Traveller-Gypsies*. Cambridge: Cambridge
                            University Press, 1983.

Puxon, G.   *The Victims*. Dublin: Aistí Éireannacha, 1967.

                            Report of the Commission on Itinerancy.
                            Dublin: Government Publications, 1963.

Rigal, J.   "Some Issues Concerning the Integration
                            of Irish Travellers", *Administration*, vol.37,
                            no.1. 1989, 87-93.

Sampson, J.   "Tinkers and their Talk", *Journal of the Gypsy
                            Lore Society*, 2. 1891, 204-21.

Seaholm, P.   "Shelta and the Creole Classification De-
                            vice". Unpublished manuscript. Austin,
                            Texas, 1977.

Taylor, D.M.   "Ethnicity and Language: a Social Psychol-
                            ogy Perspective", in *Language: Social Psycho-
                            logical Perspectives.* H.Giles, W.P.Robinson
                            and P.Smith (eds). Oxford: Pergamon Press,
                            1980.

Taylor, D.M. and   "Theoretical Contributions: a Five Stage
McKirnan, D.J.   Model of Intergroup Relations", *British
                           Journal of Social Psychology,* 23. 1984, 291-300.

Thurneysen, R.   *A Grammar of Old Irish,* trans. D.A. Binchy
                           and O.Bergin. Dublin: Institute for Ad-
                           vanced Studies, 1961.

TRAVELLERS' CANT — LANGUAGE OR REGISTER?

Dónall P. Ó Baoill,

Many contentious issues are raised by almost all who have thus far written about Travellers' Cant and I began my investigation of the Cant by asking myself several questions in the hope that my answers might clarify some of these issues. There is much disagreement amongst these writers about many of the characteristics of the Cant but the issue that has proved most contentious is the origin and age of this variety of Travellers' speech. The questions I have asked, therefore, will focus on this particular issue and if these questions are answered satisfactorily, they should clarify to some degree the salient and most important matters that should be our focus of attention in dealing with this variety of Travellers' speech. My questions can be posed briefly as follows:

(a) How old is the Cant used by Travellers and what can we say about its origin? How can we decide which of the competing theories best explains its origin?

(b) Is the creation of new words within Cant an ongoing process or has the whole process become fossilised? Does the Cant used in North America differ in this respect from what is being used in Ireland or Britain?

(c) Is the Cant a language, a dialect, a social register (see definition p.2) or do we need a new term to describe it properly? What has modern linguistic research to say about the matter? How should we approach this matter and what tools or arguments can we use in order to settle the matter one way or the other?

(d) Why didn't Travellers' Cant develop its own form of grammar, semantic expressions, social roles etc.?

(e) Are Travellers an ethnic group and what role does language and in this case the Cant play in promoting that role?

(f) How should the Cant be preserved? Should it be developed further? How? Who should do it? Should assimilation to the settled community and all that that entails be discussed in this context? What does it involve – what are the consequences for the preservation of Cant etc.?

These are important issues and must be addressed and discussed with the utmost caution and linguistic rigour at our command. This I intend to do in the following pages.

Before we step into the great quagmire of linguistic argumentation in trying to find reasonable answers to the questions we have posed above, we must first of all place our discussion within the general framework of LANGUAGE. This means that we have to talk about many important facets of language and its use.

TRAVELLER MOTHER TONGUE

The first question we must ask ourselves is – what is the mother tongue of a typical Traveller and what does he/she have to say about it? This is a most important matter for the simple reason that one's mother tongue(s) impinges to a greater or lesser extent on every aspect of the individual's development, linguistically, emotionally, mentally and educationally. Language is also important for communication both within the family/local community and with the community at large. It is also one of the strongest symbols of ethnicity and plays a major role in the education process, and success or failure in this latter domain depends to a large extent on one's command of the "school register".

It would seem from the linguistic evidence that the mother tongue of Irish Travellers is a combination of Cant and some form of Irish English. Despite the large influx of Irish vocabulary items in the Cant, I think we can safely state that Irish is not the mother tongue of the vast majority of Travellers. Since most Travellers at a certain age have some command of Irish English, no matter how basic, we must then ask ourselves how the Cant relates to their use and knowledge of that variety of English. The linguistic structure of Cant is almost entirely English – its word order is English – the means by which one asks questions is English – the grammatical endings used even on the non-English words are from English grammar (e.g. the verb endings "-ed", "-ing" and the plural "-(e)s"). Notice such phrases as **ód niucs** "two pennies" from Irish *dó* "two" and *ceann* 'head, one'; **losped** "married" from Irish *pós* "marry" + "- ed".

This then poses a certain problem for us which can be stated as follows. If a form of speech has identical grammar and structure as well as a large amount of shared vocabulary with some other language with which it has close ties and continuous contact, then we must ask whether or not we are entitled to call the former a language separate from the latter. No matter what definition of language we consult I'm afraid the answer to our question will always be in the negative. However, since the Cant has many lexical items not found in Irish English and whose origin is also vague to most of the speakers who use it daily, then perhaps we are entitled to state that the Cant is a different form of language used for specific purposes. In this respect it would not be inappropriate to call it "a register", a special form of language used on well defined occasions. It should be pointed out, however, that when one refers to "a register" one is talking about a register of some language. There are many registers used in English but what they all have in common is that the vocabulary and grammar of all such registers is English.

So where does this leave us with the Travellers' Cant? Its grammar and syntactic structure is overwhelmingly English (on the evidence of the recordings made since the middle of the nineteenth century), but a substantial part of its vocabulary and idioms are unrecognisable as anything remotely English. It is also quite obvious that the recording of Cant proved to be a most difficult task for those unfamiliar with the phonetics of Irish (language), and they state time and time again that they found it difficult to record the various nuances of pronunciation using English spellings. The recordings made by Pádraig Mac Gréine (1931-34), by Micheál Mac Éinri (1939) and by Jared Harper (1971), are exceptions and seem to capture in their different scripts (phonetics in the latter case and ordinary Irish spelling conventions in the other two) the essential phonetic characteristics of Cant. It is very clear from the former two recordings made in Ireland (in counties Longford and Mayo, respectively), that the difficulties encountered by those who recorded Cant in Britain arose in the main from the different phonetic qualities of the consonants, which are definitely Irish in origin as evidenced by such transcriptions as **gairéad** "money" from Irish *airgead,* **srochar** "key" from Irish *eochair* and **stáin** "tin" from Irish *stán.* It should also be mentioned here that the Travellers from Mayo who gave the recordings spoke Irish as well (Béaloideas IX, p.220). Thus "r" in **gairéad** is a palatalised [rj]; "ch" in **srochar** is a velar fricative [x]. The "s" in **srochar** is reported as a palatalised [sj] similar to English "sh" as in ship. These sounds and sound combinations are foreign to English and are found only in loanwords.

The question we posed some time ago is still unanswered. Since the Cant has a high percentage of English words and since its syntactic constructions and grammar are on the whole English, one might want to classify it as a register of English. However, because of its extensively Irish-based vocabulary and consequently many non-English phonetic characteristics, one might classify it as a type of "creole" created by an unusual language contact situation. One of the difficulties we face in calling it a creole is that all research on pidgins and creoles define creole as an emerging form of language which is about to take on a structure and grammar of its own. This "new language" will then become a mother tongue for those people who are descended from previous generations who spoke a more basic form of the "new language" called pidgin.

Since Cant has not developed its own grammatical and syntactic system, we are on very shaky ground if we want to describe it as a creole. It is certainly not a pidgin since it is obviously acquired as a speech system form in childhood. It is used as a means of communication amongst the Traveller community at large. Much of the variation in the pronunciation of certain words (e.g. **núspóg, múscóg, mústóg**, for example, from Irish *spúnóg* "a spoon", which is itself a loanword from English) can be shown to be the result of language learning processes as evidenced in the vast literature on first language acquisition in the last two decades. There are very strong arguments for claiming that **núspóg** is/was the original or basic form of the word in Cant and that the other two variants are derived by normal sound substitutions during childhood language acquisition. These substitutions when left unchecked emerge as alternative pronunciations. Such substitutions as [m] for [n] and [st] for [sk] are commonplace in language learning and in dialect variation.

It has its own phonetic characteristics, which is due primarily to the extensive number of Irish vocabulary items. They, in turn, account for most of its non-English lexicon, and the form in which they were acquired from Irish gives Cant its particular synchronic colouring.

PERIOD OF ORIGIN

A different question should now be posed and it is this – has there ever been a variety of Cant which did not use any English words or grammar? If such a variety had existed, it would probably have been based on an Irish substratum, since much of the extant vocabulary has been derived, albeit indirectly, from that language. Had such a variety existed, I can see no reason why it should not have survived intact as a means of communication. It is also an interesting and curious development that very few if any of what linguists call "connecting words" have been derived through Irish or any other language. Since such words are absent, there is no way in which the other lexical items can be blended together to construct larger linguistic units (clauses, sentences) within a larger discourse. This would seem to point to a situation where the overall structure of the Cant is formed outside of the structure of Irish, and that Irish words or in some instances phrases, are "borrowed" in order to replace the content words **(nouns, verbs, adjectives, adverbs)**. This leaves us with a language variety where one can ask questions, negate phrases/sentences, use different tenses and generate different clause types, only by using "words" or "connectors" from English. This may explain why the Cant has not generated a grammar and structure of its own independent of English.

If my hypothesising is correct, and it is certainly backed up by the available data, then the Cant must have been created at a time when its original speakers were bilingual, having a knowledge of both Irish and English. This would seem to date the creation as sometime in the last 350 years or so. With increasing bilingualism and continuous contact with English, the original Cant system had no time to settle and develop as a communication system. This is true in particular since most of its users have now become competent in some form of (Irish) English. One hesitates to say "monolingual" since this might prejudice the issue. However, as the number of Cant words and expressions dwindle from generation to generation (note Jared Harper's comments about this reduction of vocabulary in his paper "Gypsy Research in the South" (1971), and his comments apply equally to many Irish Travellers), there is the danger that we are dealing with monolingual speakers of some form of English with a knowledge of a restricted register which partly consists of a non-English derived lexicon which is now being pronounced with English phonetic values and encoded within a syntax and grammar that is essentially that of modern English.

There is now a great danger that the Cant may be drastically reduced and forgotten and will, therefore, cease to perform any of the functions which were up until now closely associated with it, within the Traveller community. While this would be a great pity it may be inevitable, unless we face up to the challenge and address ourselves to some of the salient issues facing Travellers and their use of Cant as an everyday form of communication, especially within some of the more integrative social domains.

IS CANT FOSSILIZED?

We must in the first instance ask ourselves why Cant words and forms are in such a fossilised state. Why isn't the creation of new words within Cant an ongoing process? All of the data collected from Ireland, Britain and the United States and Canada share a common lexicon but the Cant shows very little vitality as a living and vibrant linguistic entity, especially with regard to the creation of new vocabulary, compared to languages like English, French or Irish. Are the speakers of Cant unaware "psychologically" of the structure of those words in everyday use? Does this explain why there has been so little experimentation with the creation of new vocabulary items, although individual attempts to create a Cant form for English words such as **grandy** for **candy** in America, have been reported? Why hasn't wholesale borrowing from English taken place and why in particular have the small but important class of connectors such as conjunctions, complementisers ("that/if/whether/for" etc.), the definite and indefinite articles ("the" and "a"), remained English?. The answer would seem to point to the fact that only content words, that is words which have an inherent meaning, were borrowed, albeit in a camouflaged form, from Irish. But a speech form without innate connectors of the type mentioned above, can not, as I have pointed out earlier, develop a grammar or structure unique to itself. Thus, again we are driven to the conclusion that the Cant is but "a register", having a relatively large number of words of non-English origin, but being held together as a linguistic system by elements of English syntax and grammar.

The Cant, therefore, serves a different purpose from pidgin and creole languages. It is used mainly for communication between and within groups that share a certain background. It would seem, however, that it has not developed any styles or registers of its own. Since grammar and style carry messages for different social groups, this may pose a problem for Travellers in gaining access to types of language associated with different social levels and in particular with high-level social groupings. Thus, in the sphere of education, for example, Travellers will not be taught Cant and will have to come to terms with varieties of English they have hitherto not been accustomed to. Therefore, Travellers have a lot of catching up to do, and since language is such a powerful tool which can be misused by those in positions of authority, then clarification of the role of Cant in education and how Travellers should be exposed to (what) other varieties of English, needs to be discussed as a matter of urgency. The types of syllabi that need to be formulated, taking all the different aspects of Travellers' language backgrounds into account, should be the focus of special attention by those sensitive to all the issues involved.

In particular, we need to ask how the language of Travellers in general fits into the overall picture with regard to Irish English. Do Travellers use different varieties of English in their everyday communication, and if they do, how do they (these varieties) interact and, more importantly, what are the social functions that are attached to each variety? Where then does Traveller's Cant fit into the scheme of things? When the Cant is avoided what takes its place – general Irish English, non-standard Irish English, standard English? We know very little about such matters at the present time. Since the use of language varieties, however, is closely associated with identity and identity transfer, then there is much to be learned in sociolinguistic terms about Travellers' own views on language and language behaviour, by focusing on their own language networks and intergroup relations and by doing so to set up a linguistic data bank on which informative and sound research projects could be based.

Binchy (present volume) states that – "Grammar is not necessary for efficient communication. When pidgins develop into creoles and become a language of a closed community network, they use grammatical devices to categorise members into social groups. Grammar becomes a means of signalling membership and relative status." This implies that the existence of a community is necessary for the development of grammatical features. People must have a shared location in order for linguistic features to develop. Lexicon is the ethnic marker and grammar represents the parts of life shared with the settled community. Binchy further maintains that the small-scale Traveller daily interaction was not enough to maintain Cant grammar.

If grammar is understood in its broadest sense – the inner thread which blends the sound system, morphology, syntax and semantics of a language together – then certainly it is very necessary for effective and efficient communication. This is immediately obvious from the way in which normal languages deal with modern concepts and ideas, and even more obvious in the efforts expended by creole speakers in creating and developing an efficient language communication system. I maintain that Cant never had a grammar of its own for two main reasons, (a) it is not based entirely on Irish or English, which would have given it the potential of cultivating its own system of rules and grammar, and (b) that the linguistic changeover in Ireland, from being a monolingual Irish-speaking nation to being almost entirely monolingual English-speaking in the space of some 300 years, removed the kind of supporting environment which was necessary in order for the "new variety" to expand and develop.

The maintenance, therefore, of Traveller "ethnic" vocabulary is a crucial aspect of Traveller linguistic identity. If it is to be used efficiently in intergroup relations, it is important that it be preserved, even if in sociolinguistic terms it can not be "accurately" defined or labelled. As I have already indicated the Cant (which includes the "ethnic vocabulary" referred to above, English lexical items and a grammatical system based entirely on English) is learned by many Travellers as a form of mother tongue. This form of language is the basic means of communication amongst the Traveller community and unless it is supported and enhanced by further training especially within the educational field, then it is likely to hinder progress on a personal, social, psychological and educational level. As a form of speech it also carries with it a heavy emotional load and creates and enhances group solidarity, and, therefore, in my opinion, requires further study and research by those involved in education and related training. It deserves a symposium devoted entirely to its use in all aspects of education, job training and language therapy and clinical linguistics.

The status allocated to Cant is the key issue and much will depend on the extent that Travellers as a group want to conform or acculturate to the dominant social culture and to its speakers. We must develop a clearer picture of how Traveller language in general here in Ireland fits into the overall framework of Irish English. This cannot be done without the development of a sophisticated and open research programme dealing with Travellers' overall language usage. It is fairly obvious that Travellers use different varieties of English in their everyday communication but we have very little, if any, reliable information as to how these varieties interact and perhaps more importantly what the different social functions attached to each variety is.

In this regard it is interesting to note that very little Cant is contained in the Traveller folktales edited by George Gmelch and Ben Kroup under the title *To Shorten the Road* (1978). This is yet another aspect of Travellers' use of language which should be the subject of further research. The type of English used in the stories is cultivated to the extent that it has not been influenced to any great degree by standard English. It does of course serve a purpose but one must ask why it contains so little Cant since in essence the audience would have been Travellers by and large.

ORIGIN OF THE NON-ENGLISH ELEMENT

The question relating to the origin of the non-English element of Traveller's Cant is both complicated and contentious. I hope to address this subject on a more detailed and expanded scale in a future publication. Only in this way can this important subject be given the focus and attention it deserves within modern theoretical linguistic and sociolinguistic research. I would like, however, to draw the reader's attention to the following elements of the usage and make-up of Cant. While some of these may have been referred to in various publications, there are others that have not been touched upon. My reasons for bringing them all together here is to sharpen our focus in order that we might come to an agreement as to what the relevant linguistic features are in dealing with the subject at hand.

(i) It is fairly obvious from the phonetic variation found within different lexical items that such variation is due to processes common in language acquisition/learning and copiously reported from such studies. Relevant examples include the following:

  (a) **mústóg/múscóg/núspóg** for English "spoon". It derives from the the Irish word *spúnóg*, itself a borrowing from English with an added "*-óg*" ending. If the processes documented in Macalister (1937) are correct, then the original form of **spúnóg** in Cant was **núspóg** with the inversion or metathesis of the sounds/phonemes of the initial syllable. The other forms, therefore, are derived and are, therefore, due to (universal) processes of language acquisition which have gone unchecked, there being no "standard" to refer to. Substitutions of the type **n/m** and **sp/sc/st** are quite common in both 1st and 2nd language acquisition/learning.

  (b) **chera/therra/theddy/chini** English 'fire' from Irish "*t(e)ine/tinidh*". This interchange of 'r' and 'd' is a common consonant substitution within certain dialects of English. Recall the well known Dublin pronunciation of *delighted* as **"delira"**. This alternation can be heard in the Cant word **rodus/rorus** "door" from Irish "*doras*".

(ii) There are traces of dialectal variation in the Cant forms taken down at various times. In particular we should note the following:

  (a) Long vowels in the second syllable of such words as **núspóg** "a spoon", **tómán** "a lot, much" and **lúbín** "a loaf" from Irish *spúnóg, mórán* and *builín*, respectively. Since long vowels in non-initial syllables are shortened in Ulster Irish, then the Cant forms given above, if based originally on Irish, can only be traced to dialectal forms from Connacht or Munster Irish. Since the strongest stress or emphasis is on the first syllable of these words then the probablility is that they are of Connacht Irish origin since the Munster dialects tend to stress the second syllable in such words as *mórán* "much" and *builín* "a loaf".

(b) Irish *sparán* is **ruspán** in Cant, a form that betrays its Connacht origin. Ulster Irish has a clear "a" sound (as in English "bad") in *sparán* and, therefore, can not be the source of **ruspán**. The same word tends to be monosyllabic in Munster Irish with stress on the "-*án*" syllable. This also points to the fact that the original alterations to words *were based on pronunciation* (at least in some cases), rather than the written form.

(c) Such endings as [-**iath**] to denote Irish [-*íocht*] can certainly be traced to East Ulster dialects where words such as *scéalaíocht* "storytelling" etc., are pronounced as if there were no "*ch*" there at all. "-*ocht*/ -*acht*" is one of the endings used to derive abstract nouns in Irish. The loss of "*ch*" can be traced back to the 18th century at least since hypercorrected forms such as *slacht* for *slat* "a rod, a stick" are to be found in the literature from the East Ulster dialectal area, which in reality covers much of Ulster, including East Donegal (see O Buachalla, 1982). The form **kaihed** "a chair" once again points to an Ulster dialectal origin, since the initial syllable of Irish *cathaoir* "a chair" has a diphthong [ai] in its spoken form throughout that province. The substitution of "d" for "r" has already been alluded to.

(d) If **mark** "a bone" is from Irish *cnámh*, as seems likely, then this time we can exclude the Munster dialects since they should give a form *mank (where *denotes that this has not happened). However, in Ulster and Connacht Irish *cnámh* is pronounced *crámh*, which in all probability is the origin of **mark**. Again **ladhu, ladher, loda** "earth, dirt(y), a clay floor" from Irish *talamh* is of Connacht or Ulster origin. In these dialects "*mh*" is either dropped which gives *tala* or the ending "-*amh*" gives [u(:)] (a short or long "u"), and, hence a form /talu(:)/ is obtained. In Munster *talamh* is pronounced with a final "v", which would presumably have given *ladav.

(iii) There are also in Cant traces which show the application of universal processes/tendencies resulting in more natural/simplified sound sequences. This is seen in particular in the devoicing of b, d and g to p, t and k, respectively, in word final position. An example of this process is **klisp** "to break" from Irish *bris*. There is also a tendency to voice consonants in intervocalic position, namely, the reverse of the previous rule. The Cant word **ladu** from *talamh* as mentioned earlier is a possible example.

CONCLUSION

As I have shown above, there is quite an amount of dialectal information to be gleaned from the transcription of Cant words as captured by various investigators. There is also a certain amount of evidence which shows that the non-English derived vocabulary of Cant has undergone definite universal processes similar or identical to those which have been reported from language acquisition/learning studies and from the studies of various informal registers in different languages. In order to ascertain the origin of the extensive vocabulary items of Cant, which are not readily accessible to English speakers, we must first of all isolate all the other influences which have given Cant its present shape. This study is a prerequisite if we are to clear the way for a full investigation, which will hopefully lead us in a logical and clear thinking manner to the origin of the "indigenous" vocabulary of Cant. Had I tried to do this here, the space allotted would not do justice to the subject or the detailed arguments that this type of research entails. Therefore, I hope to take up the subject in the near future in a more extended publication than has been possible here.

In conclusion, may I add that what is really important now is not the origin of Cant, whatever it may be, but its FUTURE. In this respect Travellers themselves must decide how they want it developed, cultivated, taught in schools and extended in a way that will make it an integral part of their own self-identity in every sphere of their daily lives. In this way, they will have handed on in a safe and reasonably permanent form, a part of their heritage of which they can all be proud. It is only by getting to know *what Cant is, including all its weaknesses and strengths,* and with the help perhaps of educationalists and linguistic research in particular, that this can be achieved. Let's hope that the debate can now begin.

REFERENCES

Arnold, Frederick S.
"Our Old Poets and the Tinkers", *Journal of American Folklore,* Vol. II. 1898, 210-220.

Cash, Anthony
"The Language of the Maguires", *Journal of the Gypsy Lore Society,* 4th Series, Vol. 1, No. 3. 1977, 177-181.

Cleeve, Brian
"The Secret Language", *Studies,* Autumn 1983, 252-263.

Gmelch, George and Kroup, Ben
To Shorten The Road – Traveller Folktales from Ireland. Dublin: The O'Brien Press, 1978.

Harper, Jared
"Gypsy Research in the South", in *The Not So Solid South: Anthropological Studies in Regional Subculture.* J. Kenneth Morland (ed.). Southern Anthropological Society Proceedings No. 4. University Georgia Press, 1971.

Harper, Jared and Hudson, Charles
"Irish Traveller Cant", *Journal of English Linguistics,* 1971, 78-86.

Macalister, R.A.S.   *The Secret Languages of Ireland: With special reference to the origin and nature of the Shelta language, partly based upon the collections and manuscripts of the late John Sampson.* 8vo, Cambridge, 1937, 248.

Mac Éinrí, Mícheál   "'Ceant' agus Saoghal na dTincéirí", *Béaloideas*, Iml. IX, Uimhir II, 1939, 219-229.

Mac Gréine, Pádraig   "Irish Tinkers or 'Travellers'. Some Notes on their Manners and Customs, and their secret language or 'Cant'". *Béaloideas III.* 1931, 170-186. 1932, 290-303. *Béaloideas IV,* 1934, 259-263.

Meyer, Kuno   "On the Irish Origin and Age of Shelta", *Gypsy Lore Society Journal II.* 1891, 257-266.

Ó Buachalla, Breandán   "On the Historical Roots of the Philology/Linguistics Controversy", *Papers from the 5th International Conference on Historical Linguistics* (Amsterdam Studies in the Theory and History of Linguistic Science: Series IV – Current Issues in Linguistic Theory. Volume 21). Anders Ahlqvist (ed.). John Benjamins Publishing Company, 1982.

Sampson, John   "Tinkers and their Talk", *Gypsy Lore Society Journal II,* 1881, 204-221.

"Shelta, or Shelru", *Chambers' Encyclopaedia,* Vol. IX, 1893, 389.

"A Hundred Shelta Sayings" [in the Ulster dialect], *Gypsy Lore Society Journal I,* 1908, 272-277.

A VIEW FROM NORTHERN IRELAND

Paul Noonan

A number of contributors to the present volume have drawn attention to the arguments about Travellers' status as an essentially political one. An analysis of the situation of Travelling People in Ireland, which takes as its starting point the ethnicity of Travellers, must in very short order reach the conclusion that the main obstacle to the full expression of this ethnicity and the cause of the majority of problems facing Travellers is the racism of the dominant settled society.

Those who do not accept Travellers as an ethnic group have usually inverted this relationship and have viewed Travellers from a pathological perspective which blames them as "deviants", "drop-outs", "failed settled people" or a culture of poverty. In short, Travellers are seen as a problem. Central and local government policies which have traditionally been based on this analysis have sought either (a) to harass and oppress Travellers or (b) to assimilate them.

The first type of policy, i.e. harassment, is still very much a reality in Northern Ireland as evictions in Armagh, Belfast and Craigavon and Newry in recent times have shown, as well as the omnipresent piles of clay and boulders dumped by authorities on traditional camps.

All Travellers in receipt of Social Fund benefits are required to sign at 11.00 a.m. on Thursday mornings throughout Northern Ireland. The Department of Health and Social Services has recently claimed that this administrative measure is not in fact a discriminatory one based on an assumption of widespread benefit fraud among the Traveller community, but is in fact for the Travelling community's own convenience! As if the measure was introduced following a piece of consumer-sensitive market research!

The second, assimilationist, type of policy, too, is still alive and well north of the Border. Comments contained in The Government Advisory Committee on Travellers (A.C.T.) interim findings on a 1988 survey of Travellers in the North reveal the mindset we are all too familiar with.

A number of the survey's questions asked Travellers if they wished to continue with a travelling lifestyle or if there were members of their families who wished to live in the settled community (if so they were asked to give names, ages, relationships etc). To the obvious disappointment of some members of the government committee Travellers wanted to remain Travellers, and I quote from the report:

"A common theme running through the responses is that travellers [sic] are committed to their lifestyle and, with only very few exceptions, intend to continue as travellers. The hope has been expressed within A.C.T. that if the travellers are given good standards of serviced sites, then some, particularly those in the younger age group, having experienced an intermediate form of 'settled' living might decide to give up travelling.

There is, as yet, no evidence of the likelihood of that trend but with the on-going development of serviced sites, it might eventually happen when those sites are well established and become familiar to the travellers. On the face of it, the travellers intend to continue as travellers."

Elsewhere in this volume, Michael McDonagh has described how nomadism is the key element of Traveller culture particularly in relation to economic and social life and how denial of nomadism leads to serious psychological and social problems (comparable to those faced elsewhere by other peoples in the world whose culture has been oppressed such as Native Americans and Australian Aborigines).

Article 13 of the United Nations Universal Declaration of Human Rights states that "Everyone has the right to freedom of movement and residence within the borders of each state", yet Northern Ireland has introduced "designation" through the Miscellaneous Provisions Order N.I. (1985). This law effectively imposes a quota of Travellers to a particular area if a local authority can satisfy the Department of the Environment that "adequate" provision has been made for Travellers who "normally" reside in or "resort to" the district. Once an area is designated, Travellers not camped on serviced sites will be evicted at short notice. In effect, whole areas can be declared off-limits to Travellers, in direct contradiction of Article 13 of the U.N. Charter.

At the instigation of the Department of the Environment, one or two government departments have introduced a "Toleration Policy". A dictionary defines the word 'toleration' in the following terms: "To endure, permit, allow to exist, be practiced etc". The word implies that one party puts up with something that it does not itself like from another party. It is an unequal relationship which the dominant or more powerful party can decide to end at any time, it is a relationship of patronage, not one in which both parties have equal and complementary rights.

The Toleration Policy reads as follows:

"Travellers who encamp on Departmental land should be allowed to do so subject to the following conditions.

—   *that no permanent or transit facility for Travellers has been established within the District Council area.*

—   *that occupation does not constitute a measurable public health hazard or cause pollution to water supplies.*

—   *that occupation does not create a traffic hazard.*

—   *that occupation does not create a right to long term use of the site. The situation should be reviewed at regular intervals not exceeding three months.*

—   *that the Department has no current or immediate use for the land.*

— *that there is no excessive overcrowding and that the area is kept in a clean and tidy condition.*

— *that the Travellers behave in a reasonable and orderly manner* (Advisory Comm. Final Report 1989, App. 3)."

The interpretation of this exhaustive set of pre-conditions of course is discretionary. Most public bodies do not even bother to adhere to these rules, and evict Traveller families as they like with impunity. Yet less than half of Traveller families in Northern Ireland are accommodated on permanent serviced sites. In Belfast, where 40% of Travellers live, the City Council has only completed a twenty family serviced site sixteen years after voting in favour of doing so. Some of the existing serviced sites are gerry-built and resemble ghettos.

The diffuse non-formalised power and control structures within the Traveller Community (typical of nomadic groups) have proved particularly taxing to our perplexed authorities, who have remained persistently impervious to the idea of full, meaningful and systematic consultation with Travellers about site and other social provision. The views of these people can be summed up by the recent comments of an official employed by the Department of the Environment to draft plans for sites in Belfast when he stated "It's in the Travellers' nature to be un-cooperative". (The real reason why the Travellers were being un-cooperative with this official was because he was trying to foist on them a temporary site with third rate facilities which Travellers believed would become permanent).

Despite widespread and profound ignorance of Traveller culture, most government and local authority departments have presumed to know what is best for Travellers. On occasion these authorities have attempted to disguise their paternalism with the fig-leaf of tokenism – the token Traveller or few Travellers are informed what provision will be made for them, usually on the agency's premises, on the agency's terms, often in incomprehensible jargon. In other words the situation is totally weighted against Travellers having a chance to put their views, while the ears of settled officials are often closed to them anyway.

Ethnocentric ignorance is manifest in the latest government report on Travelling People (Advisory Comm. Final Report 1989). I shall cite a few examples:

(i)   "Travellers' culture has no tradition of education and no experience of sending children to school regularly. There has been little or no incentive beyond the desire to have children prepared for the First Communion or Confirmation" (p. 10, para. 5.1). This statement ignores the crucially important informal education the Traveller child receives within the family, while it does not make reference to the reasons for the **apparent** lack of interest in formal education i.e. enforced movement through eviction, ethnocentric and irrelevant curriculum and teaching methods etc.

(ii) In the section of the report dealing with "Community Relations", the churches are charged with "bridging the gap" between the Traveller and settled communities, while the role of the state in relation to community relations, discrimination and racism is conspicuous by its total absence (p. 15, para. 9.21). In which other nation states are churches charged with the protection of the rights of ethnic minorities?

(iii) The report urges that "Education of Travellers should include specific training in citizenship to instil in them a sense of their own worth in society at large and the reciprocal obligations required of them in their behaviour towards their fellow citizens". There is no reference to the education of those fellow citizens who are ultimately responsible for the racist oppression of the Traveller community. The conclusion must be that the blame lies with the victim (p. 15, para.9.23).

(iv) Comments in the report on Travellers' health did not focus on the effect of unserviced sites as the primary cause of Travellers' poor health profile, but instead emphasised the secondary (though important) factor of lack of access to health service, while a third of the section raised the diversionary and inadequately researched issue of genetic factors (pp. 12-13).

(v)   Finally, the government report **does** state that "A.C.T. in all its recommendations has taken into account that Travellers are an ethnic group", but **does not** draw the appropriate conclusion that it is widespread racism, including institutional racism, which oppresses the expression of that ethnicity (p. 14). Institutional racism, by which I mean "the policies of institutions that work to perpetuate racial inequality without acknowledging that fact" is not adequately addressed. Institutional racism can be deliberate or unconscious, overt or covert but its effects are an indictment of the injustice of state policy towards Travellers – these effects include a literacy rate of around 15%, refusal of admission to Travellers in some schools, no Travellers at secondary or third level education, a life expectancy of 50 years, high infant mortality rates, high rates of hospitalisation for children; widespread lack of access or differential access to a whole range of state services.

Institutional racism can only be addressed following the recognition by agencies that it exists and by the adoption of specific policies aimed at taking affirmative action including the adoption of anti-racist policies.

Typical of many of the recommendations is the following gem! "Every opportunity should be taken to heighten awareness that Travellers are a distinct ethnic group with special needs". But the report does not indicate who should undertake this task, how it might be done, and whether there should be an obligation to do so. Failure to address the issue of racism and institutional racism is no less than connivance in the perpetuation of its effects.

A report by another government agency in Northern Ireland, the Standing Advisory Committee on Human Rights, has recently begun to address the legislative issue (1990). The S.A.C.H.R.'s Report draws attention to the protection of minorities under international law. The United Nations Covenant on Economic and Social Rights and the International Covenant on Civil and Political Rights both provide for self-determination as follows:

"All peoples have the right of self-determination. By virtue of that right they freely determine their political status, and freely pursue their economic, social and cultural development".

The report notes a growing trend towards a recognition of the close relationship between the concept of self-determination and of group rights within the state. For example, Article 27 of the International Covenant on Civil and Political Rights, which is binding on the U.K. as a signatory, states:

"That in those states in which ethnic, religious or linguistic minorities exist, persons belonging to such minorities shall not be denied the right, in community with the other members of their group, to enjoy their own culture, to profess and practise their religion or to use their own language".

A number of other protections for minorities within existing states are currently being discussed or drafted, e.g.

– The "Draft Declaration on the Rights of Minorities" (United Nations)

– The "Charter for Rights of Ethnic Minorities" (European Community).

The Committee recognises that:

"There is a substantial body of opinion among those concerned with human rights which accepts that the granting or recognition of some special rights for members of minority groups within established state boundaries is legitimate under international human rights law and that such provisions may occasionally be required".

The Committee concludes that the rights of the two main communities be included within a new Northern Ireland Constitution Act.

Travellers' right to be nomadic, curtailed by the Miscellaneous Provisions Order 1985, Part IV Article 9 (allowing for designation and effectively providing for a quota of Travellers within any given area in Northern Ireland), should be protected in any new constitution and I call upon the Advisory Committee for Travellers to promote the introduction of such a measure if they are to be seen as serious about Travellers' status as an ethnic group.

The S.A.C.H.R. report cites Mandla v Dowell Lee (1983) in which Lord Fraser defined the following criteria for ethnicity:

1. A long shared history, of which the group is conscious as distinguishing it from other groups, and the memory of which keeps it alive.

2. A cultural tradition of its own, including family and social customs and manners often but not necessarily associated with religious observance. In addition to these two essential characteristics a number of other characteristics were seen as relevant.

3. Either a common geographical origin or descent from a small number of common ancestors.

4. A common language, not necessarily peculiar to the group; a common literature peculiar to the group.

5. A common religion different from that of neighbouring groups or from the general community surrounding it.

6. Being a minority or being an oppressed or dominant group within a larger community.

The S.A.C.H.R. report concludes from this that:

"The criteria expressed in Mandla v Dowell Lee might, however, have direct relevance in Northern Ireland in respect of members of the travelling community", and further:

"S.A.C.H.R. recommends that a Race Relations (Northern Ireland) Act or Order parallel to that in Great Britain should be introduced without delay", (and indicates that it can be introduced at the "stroke of a pen" without major difficulty). The report has been with Secretary of State since June 1990. I wish to take this opportunity both to endorse the recommendations of S.A.C.H.R. and call upon the Northern Ireland Office to introduce the measure without further delay.[2]

NOTES

[1]   The S.A.C.H.R. is an agency charged with advising the government on the adequacy and effectiveness of the law in relation to discrimination.

[2]   In December 1992, the Central Community Relations Unit of the Northern Ireland Office issued a consultative document or Green Paper on "Race Relations in Northern Ireland" in which the government stated that it is prepared to consider whether "Traditional Irish Travellers" should be recognised as an ethnic group and specifically covered by any proposed race legislation for Northern Ireland. *Race Relations in Northern Ireland.* Central Community Relations Unit, December 1992.

REFERENCES

Central Community Relations Unit. *Race Relations in Northern Ireland.* Belfast: Northern Ireland Office, December 1992.

Government Advisory Committee on Travellers (Northern Ireland). *Interim Findings on a Survey of Travellers in Northern Ireland.* Belfast: Department of the Environment for Northern Ireland, 1988.

Government Advisory Committee on Travellers (Northern Ireland). *Final Report of the Advisory Committee on Travellers (N.I.) for the period 1 August 1986 – 31 December 1989.* Belfast: Department of the Environment for Northern Ireland, 1989.

Local Government (Miscellaneous Provisions) (Northern Ireland) Order. Belfast: H.M.S.O., 1985.

Standing Advisory Committee on Human Rights. *Religious and Political Discrimination and Equality of Opportunity in Northern Ireland.* Belfast: H.M.S.O., June 1990.

FINAL THOUGHTS: A CASE FOR CELEBRATION?

Mairin Kenny

In this contribution, Mairin Kenny analyses the dynamics at work in the original Conference and identifies some themes running through it and tasks facing participants.

The Conference on "Irish Travellers: History, Culture, Ethnicity" was an academic event with a difference: the subjects of study were active and critical contributors. Travellers and sedentary people (comprising academics, and others involved with Travellers) were present so there were not so many questions answered as answers questioned; and the challenge went both ways. "Bringing it all back home" proved to be at once a rigorous and challenging academic task, and a politically important one. In this final contribution I will comment, from the perspective of my own experience in research and teaching, on some themes which I think were significant and which reveal tasks that remain to be done. I must state at the outset that being sedentary myself, I will often refer to sedentary people as "we", to Travellers as "you".

That Travellers are an ethnic group was accepted by most as a given, and the tensions between speakers, whether from platform or floor, were within that framework. Papers presented dealt with various aspects of Travellers' ethnic identity, revealing a richness and depth of data and awakening an awareness that in the Traveller-sedentary divide there lies an ancient and profound human phenomenon – one that has been hitherto unnoticed, negated or, as speakers attested, misconstructed in both academic and policy-making circles. Yet the flaws in thinking which surfaced in the debate within the Conference itself can be traced back to this very divide. Judith Okely, in the opening paper, spoke of internal colonialism: the concept provides a tool for analysis of the process of the Conference which both illuminates that process and reveals the tasks that need to be undertaken.

I would like, for a moment, to reflect again on the historic and current nature of the colonial relationship in question. Colonisation in the case of sedentary-Traveller relations takes a special shape. The core value of Traveller culture, much talked about during the Conference, is nomadism – meaning, not necessarily the intention to keep travelling, but the nomadic mindset. However, this core value has been problematised by the dominant sedentary society: Travellers have historically been useful but unwanted and marginalised. In the process the dominant sedentary group has taken nomadism – this core of Traveller culture – and turned it into a key instrument of their oppression, ensuring that forced movement is the only experience of nomadism most Travellers have. Almost all their discourse about travel is shaped as a result by this experience (that this negative transformation is not complete is an indicator of their cultural resilience). This situation gives particular moral urgency to the need to examine language used in relation to both groups. For a start, I use the term "sedentary" people, not "settled" people in referring to us; I suggest that this shift is significant: "settled" has moral connotations – we settle down, settle up, even the Traveller child who is happy in school has settled in. "Sedentary" has no such overtones.

Not only have we delegitimised nomadism: sedentary society has also colonised the cultural space of nomadic people by taking over, for instance, their wisdom traditions and interpreting them in the light of its own experience, making that interpretation the norm: the Old Testament for instance was the book of a nomadic people; pilgrimages are important as ways of purification in many religious traditions; and sedentary discourse is full of metaphors of travel: in psychological/spiritual growth, we go on journeys of discovery (even second ones), we move on, we progress; in talking about striving towards a goal we often use the term a "long haul".

We do not advert to the possibility that Travellers relate to these images differently from sedentary people. In our history teaching (I confess as a practising teacher) we present sedentarisation as an improvement on nomadism and as a precondition for the development of high culture: people were nomadic until the smart ones discovered crops, didn't have to travel any more, could develop surpluses, free people to become specialists, build cities, develop high culture. We never advert to the evidence that nomads also had, and have, their own specialists and high culture.

To return to the Conference: a pull-push process occurred in the overall debate: sedentary people pulled back, revealing the cultural terrain (wrong word for a nomadic people?) of the Travellers; and Travellers pushed forwards, claiming it. But did we yield it up? We showed ourselves to be caught up in a post-colonial dynamic – we the power-holders, the sedentary people, still with a coloniser mind-set; the Travellers with a colonised one. Where the power lay was evident in the drift of the debate, for all our struggle, on both sides, to be free. The agenda of the sedentary dominated. Flaws in our sedentary perspective were named as racist and unfounded and were laid to rest: for instance exoticism in our attitude to Gypsies as opposed to Travellers (the former came – though, oh dear, not last year without a visa – from ancient India, whereas the latter were mere locals), but those flaws resurrected themselves, particularly in relation to history and language. It is worth reflecting on the process.

We were repeatedly told that myths of origin did not really matter to Travellers, that Travellers adopt and adapt such myths in a variable, strategic way; that they regard such as "baggage": that questions of ancientness/roots do not fit into the meaning systems of many commercial nomads such as Travellers, who find their sense of validity in a vital network of relationships rather than in a sense of ancient historicity. Yet we continually returned to debating where they came from. Likewise, we concentrated on the age of the Traveller language, and did not debate alternative criteria for measuring its validity provided by speakers such as Alice Binchy, who spoke of its functional value in a fragmented nomadic society, and its significance for the users as an ethnic marker both within and without their community.

I would like to make two comments on this. The first is that by allowing this question of age, of origin, to dominate the debate we accorded to it such status that any attempt to shift to another perspective becomes tainted with an aura of escapism, appears weak, less legitimate. Other valid ways of approaching the question of the validity of the Traveller claim to ethnicity, of the validity of their language were indicated. Why did we not work with these, if not because we ourselves are still unconsciously ethnocentric as researchers? Secondly, I would suggest that in the process of our debate we sedentary people displayed something of the coloniser mindset, in allowing our will to permanence to dominate the discussion. If this will to permanence, which is perhaps peculiar to sedentary people, dominates the structure of the debate, then our de-colonising of the cultural space of nomads has a long way to go. (In another context we might call the will to permanence peculiarly male: it reflects perhaps shared characteristics of two ancient power divisions: women/men; nomads/sedentarists.

Tasks await each group represented at the Conference – the academics and the policy-makers/practitioners (almost all sedentary people in these two groups at the moment); and the Travellers. The tasks can de defined in the terms used by the anthropologist Clifford Geertz[1] when speaking of newly independent nationalist states, who he says find themselves caught in a tension between holding to inherited patterns, and moving with changing times – impelled in short to consider two questions: who are we; and where do we fit in? The same questions await emergent ethnic groups. These terms continue the analysis of colonial practice, applicable to Ireland as a state, and to Travellers as an ethnic group within it. Ireland focussed on the first question in the movement towards and early days of independence, reviving the Irish language, reasserting our cultural traditions in dance, sports etc.; the need to attend to the second grew due to political thinking, economic pressure, emigration, the media, and feelings of being imprisoned in a mausoleum-like concept of

Irishness (Brown, 1981); the debate goes on. However, in the early days of the Travellers' emergence as a people in Ireland, their own struggles with these questions went unnoticed: they were "spoken for" – in the '60s the dominant sedentary group felt no need to ask who are the Travellers; rather we sought to determine where do we fit them in. This chain of colonising relationships shaping Irish society is continually changing, breaking, and re-forming: we here are acting in it, and so Geertz's questions are very useful.

The attitudes of the '60s are far from being a thing of the past, but inroads have been made into our complacency; this Conference has continued the process. Patricia McCarthy in her courageous and thoughtful paper laid to rest one old model of Travellers – that they belong to a sub-culture of poverty (a perception for which her original research was made to carry too much of the blame: it hardly caused, but rather was invoked as a rationale for, the thinking of the dominant group, many of whom probably never read her work). As indicated by Paul Noonan, statutory bodies and their employees both North and South operate – usually unconsciously – on the basis of this and other models of Travellers, such as that they are drop-outs, people down on their luck who will rejoin, given the chance; or that they are exotic (also debunked here); or that they are just like the rest of us. These models – which implicitly normalise and universalise sedentarism, trivialise nomadism, and ignore the problematic relationship between them – provide the base for "solutions" which have themselves turned out to be problematic for both Traveller and sedentary people. Now the question of identity is asserting itself, demanding attention: Travellers have been placed into what we saw as the modern world for them, and the question of who they are is now challenging that mis-fit.

So I would say the question "who are the Travellers?" is a key one, and is at the core of the tasks that arose for us from this Conference. Since the balance of power – and therefore the main onus for change – rests with sedentary people, our task comes first (however, I will leave the academic task – because this was an academic Conference – till last). Above all we must confront the racism in our own society – but that is easily said. Unless we come to recognise on the one hand our own ethnocentrism, and on the other the distinctive nature of Traveller identity, how it is constructed and how it is changing, we cannot recognise the real nature of the racism.

The core of our task is a shift in mindset. This shift which we practitioners/policy-makers must make is very simple in a way, but profound. We underestimate the extent of our ethnocentrism (remember the pro-sendentarist bias in the history we learned/teach). We can easily miss evidence of nomadism in what is under our noses. For instance, I only recently paid serious attention to the form of the verb "to go" which Traveller children habitually use, and to which we, their teachers, often give idiosyncratic status by using it humorously ourselves: they use "go on" where we would use "go" – as in "they've gone on out of the house"; "X isn't in school today – she's gone on": "I'm going on out of this place". From an informal survey, it seems that this form of the verb to go in this context is common among Travellers in many areas. This may sound trivial, but I would argue otherwise. The form "go on" denotes continuation or resumption – of education (going on to university); of talk ("please go on"/"X goes on and on"). I think we sedentary people use this form in relation to movement in calling for resumption of interrupted progress (as after a rest-stop on a walk), or to avoid such interruption; otherwise we "go, go off/back/to/ from . . .", but, if my observations are right, Travellers use it constantly when talking of any movement from place to place. I suggest that Travellers are also referring to continuing a journey; and that, constantly embedded as it is in the most ordinary conversational interactions, this usage could be a significant indicator of a nomadic mindset, indicating an ever-present sense of being on the move. Equally significantly, we sedentary workers never gave it any thought (I found I am not the only one to have sinned), despite adopting the usage in our own talk.

We must examine the model of Travellers which shapes our perceptions, causing us to miss and misread a variety of phenomena, and perhaps even their entire cultural base. Changes in that practice – which we are being called on to make anyway – will appear baffling as long as we remain in our familiar ethnocentric mindset. The shift in that mindset is comparable to that demanded in addressing issues related to the inclusion of women: what was assumed to be the natural order of things was found to be a male construct; it was not enough to simply make room within it for women. We need to realise that there is nothing particularly natural about our sedentary lifestyles and all that they require, any more than there is about reading from left to right.

The Conference was not about the content of the issues involved in our areas of work, such as what forms of accommodation, education, or health care should be on offer, or how to deal with residents' hostility to sites etc.; rather it called us to consider some aspects of Traveller culture which indicate the need for a change in practice. We have consistently undervalued the need to listen and learn before acting. Take, for instance, issues relating to the economic base of Travellers – characterised, as Sinéad Ní Shúinéar said, by flexibility facilitated by nomadism – and how this relates to their accommodation needs: recent history shows we do not know what secure accommodation or viable economic structures for nomadic people might be. Our difficulty with Traveller economy and accommodation is linked to failure to legitimise nomadism itself: this is evident in the chronic failure to take commercial nomadism as an economic way of life into account in the location of sites. In order to understand and act appropriately, we need to listen to Travellers, but this includes recognising the silencing of their traditions which their delegitimation has imposed: as an integral part of listening we must allow them opportunities to undo internal and internalised colonialism, we must return to them the space to come to terms with their experience and to find their voice.

To address Travellers: during the Conference you pushed forward and claimed your heritage, proved you can no longer be named by us, as happened when we coined the name "Itinerant" and you accepted it. But colonial practices and racism have not just produced the directly related exclusion practices and appalling living conditions which many suffer. A number of Travellers who spoke referred to the persistence of internalised oppression, producing in members or sections of their people a lack of confidence in or ambivalence about their identity. As a teacher I must say that many if not most Traveller children show depressed levels of academic achievement. This is not all due to lazy racist teachers or oppressive school structures, though these are highly significant; the cause must also be sought in the pupils' often extremely low self-image and ambivalence about identity.

Within the terms of the Conference the task indicated for Travellers is to continue to undo this, by addressing yourselves to the question who are we? Until recently, two kinds of campaign tactic relating to the exclusion experienced by Travellers have held the forefront: a push to undo structural injustice and racism, and statements of victimage; statements of cultural distinctiveness of Travellers were made but not explored. I think it is urgent that, along with the structural analysis, along with the assertion of rights and the fight against racism, there must go celebration of identity, else absorption could result. Absorption is a form of racism which can be imposed on people who have not named and claimed their distinctiveness, and when problems ensue, the victims, who after all wanted to be included/treated like everyone else, can again be blamed for not "fitting in". Less adequate again are campaigns centred on statements of victimage: while these are justified and powerful strategic tools, they also do not provide an alternative to models of Travellers currently held by many sedentary people, hostile and friendly; and they clearly do not provide a healthy basis for a sense of identity for Travellers. Given the ambivalence about identity spoken of at the Conference, I suggest that there is a danger that these campaign discourses – responses to the actions of the dominant society – can do their work too well and become the whole story for both sedentary and Traveller people.

Celebration of identity is, by contrast, autonomous and empowering: it is welcomed, as for instance at the opening of the Conference, when the then Minister for Labour, Bertie

Ahern, spoke of the new confidence in their identity which he found in young Travellers (and it raises a lot of heat in some quarters where Traveller-as-victim was accepted). The pilgrimages to Máméan and Tobar an Ailt, mentioned by Michael McDonagh; the work of the Irish Traveller Movement; Traveller voices on their own radio programmes, and in the Channel 4 television programme; the growing national Travelling Women's Forum; the newly revived interest in the language: all are celebrations of the strength and resilience of a culture being maintained by an increasingly threatened, delicate and fragmented network of people. I would suggest – and I think what Michael and others presented bears it out – that such celebration of identity is essential to progress towards equality. As with the Irish historically, the questions remain: when you have got free of the oppressor, when in the best of all possible worlds you have got rid of the racism and gained your rights: who are you then? And without an answer to that question, how can the struggle be successful?

Finally, the task for academics. It is a fact that for the near future at least – until racism in formal education and its effects on Traveller participation are overcome (the educators' first task) – most academics in this area will be sedentary people. Our tasks come quickly to mind from the experience of the Conference – from for instance the constant search for answers within familiar parameters. As researchers we could note that the work done by any group in presenting their myths of origin is that of validating/celebrating their identity: in the mixed and (for us) too-variable myths Travellers present us, they celebrate their strategic flexibility. In this as in many other facets of research into Travellers, we could perhaps expect that where strategic flexibility is the mode, uncertainty and tentativeness might be the appropriate academic response. We could also note the need to approach Traveller language from a different standpoint; and reflect again on the dangers to which research succumbs in taking on the subculture of poverty model. I suggest that we must engage in committed research: I believe that there is a moral imperative involved here, given the racist nature of the situation. We must serve the people, dialogue with Travellers and those working with Travellers in relation to our choice of topics and methods, and our research findings – not to pander to either partitioners or Travellers, but to do research which will, as appropriate validate or challenge both groups. Indeed, given the surprise of many (all?) of us at the range and substance of the issues dealt with at this Conference, we academics will be challenged as much as that world out there.

So, what is there to celebrate? That we, sedentary and Traveller, are on a long journey; that in the process we will find out who we both are, and (provided place is understood flexibly!):

. . . the end of all our exploring/Will be to arrive where we started/And know the place for the first time.

(T.S. Eliot: Four Quartets).

NOTES

[1]   Terence Brown outlines and applies Geertz's theory in *Ireland, a Social and Cultural History*. Glasgow: Fontana, 1981, 181-2.

CONTRIBUTORS

THOMAS ACTON
D.Phil. Ran the first Gypsy Council Caravan Summer School in England in 1967, and is now Reader in Romani Studies, University of Greenwich, London.

ALICE BINCHY
Joint Chairperson South Dublin Travellers' Support Group. Currently revising D. Phil. thesis on *The Status and Functions of Shelta* for Oxford University.

MARTIN COLLINS
Irish Traveller. Community Youth Worker with Dublin Travellers' Education and Development Group (DTEDG).

MAIRIN KENNY
Headmistress, St. Kieran's Special School for Travellers, Bray, Co. Wicklow. Doctoral research student, Sociology Department, Trinity College Dublin.

DONALD KENRICK
Ph.D. Author of *The Destiny of Europe's Gypsies*. Adviser to Romany Guild.

MAY McCANN
Ph.D. Department of Social Anthropology, The Queen's University of Belfast.

PATRICIA McCARTHY
M.Soc.Sc. Social Worker with Dublin County Council. Author of reports and articles on homelessness and on Irish Travellers.

MICHAEL McDONAGH
Irish Traveller. Community Worker. Employed as National Coordinator for Accommodation for Travellers by the National Council for Travelling People.

DYMPNA McLOUGHLIN

Ph.D. Historical geographer with special interest in nine-teenth-century Irish social history.

SINÉAD NÍ SHÚINÉAR

M.A. Anthropology (Kraków). Thesis and subsequent research on Irish Travellers.

PAUL NOONAN

Formerly Coordinator of NI Council for Travelling People, and research and development worker with the West Belfast Traveller Project for Save the Children Fund. Currently Director of Belfast Travellers' Education and Development Group (BTEDG)

DÓNALL Ó BAOILL

Ph.D. Head, Structural Linguistics Section, Institiúid Teangeolaíochta Éireann.

JOHN O'CONNELL

M.A. (Econ). Director, Dublin Travellers' Education and Development Group (DTEDG).

SÉAMAS Ó SÍOCHÁIN

Ph.D. Department of Anthropology, St. Patrick's College, Maynooth, Co. Kildare

JUDITH OKELY

D.Phil. Department of Social Anthropology, University of Edinburgh. Author of *Traveller Gypsies* and co-author of *Gypsies and Government Policy in England*.

JOSEPH RUANE

M.A. Department of Sociology, University College Cork.

INDEX